STUDY AND EX

CERTIFIED PROFESSIONAL CODER (CPC) EXAM

The *Official Genius Exam Coaches*™ Edition

- Designed for crammers
- Strategic and concise study guide
- Genius Exam Coaches prompts

DR. VINCE MIKAEL POWERS

CONTENTS

GENIUS EXAM COACHES™(GEC™) INTRODUCTION

Welcome to the Genius Exam Coaches™ (GEC™) Study Guide program! The approach is based on the learning program designed by Dr. Artyom Zinchenko (Ph.D. in Cognitive and Neuroscience) and Dr. Wallace Panlilio II (Ph.D. in Educational Psychology). Their program is based on thousands of hours of combined research on optimal learning and helps you achieve the best possible test results. What sets GEC apart from other test preparation programs is that it is designed for crammers or people who have very limited time to review for an exam. The book's structure and design incorporate the most recent and most promising techniques from the area of educational experimental psychology and neuroscience, which should speed up and solidify learning experience. So how can you get the most out of the GEC program?

First, we encourage you to answer the GEC Learning Questionnaire found on the next page—our questionnaire highlights various learning factors, such as motivation, attitude, and strategies. Answering the questionnaire will help you prepare for your test more holistically. You will be able to establish a solid foundation as you prepare for your exam.

Second, as you go over the books, you will find that there will be questions at the top section of each page. The questions will prompt you to recall or reflect on the subject matter. The goal is to reinforce your knowledge and develop critical thinking skills. Instead of rereading, you must try to remember and reflect on what you have learned first, even if you have to struggle at first. The effort is an essential part of the learning process. You interrupt the learning process if you immediately reread whenever you struggle to remember. Do your best to delay finding the answer. Doing so will be well worth it.

Third, you will also find questions asking you to reflect on your learning approach, including your motivation, attitude, and strategies. Being mindful of one's learning process is essential to ensuring that how you learn continues to be optimal.

Do not be surprised when the questions are about the previous chapters' concepts. This approach is intentional because this will dramatically reinforce a deeper knowledge about the topic and make you familiar with uncertainties when you encounter complex and confusing questions in the exam.

Finally, there will be a checklist at the end of each chapter. We encourage you to take the time to mentally recall each item, then elaborate on what you have learned by writing or talking about your insights or even discussing what you have learned with your peers. The more you write or talk about it, the more connections your brain cells can establish about such a topic. As a result, you will have a stronger foundation for better results in your exam.

GENIUS EXAM COACHES™ (GEC™) QUESTIONNAIRE

1. Why are you studying for this exam?

2. How will passing this exam impact your life?

3. How can you motivate yourself to study even if you don't feel like studying?

4. How can you reduce, if not eliminate, the different distractions like phones, emails, social media, internet, among others?

5. What are your daily, weekly, or monthly learning objectives?

6. How can you manage your time to help you achieve your objectives?

7. How can you organize your study environment to help you achieve your objectives?

8. How often can you mentally recall and elaborate on what you have learned?

9. How often can you write test items for you to answer as part of your mock test simulation?

10. Can you take a step back before, during, and after your study period to assess how you're learning in order to ensure that you're learning effectively?

INTRODUCTION

The Role

Generally referred to as a medical records and health information technologist, a certified professional coder is a skilled member of the healthcare industry. In this position, you will be responsible for arranging and keeping medical records for your employer and clients. A coder serves as the point of contact between billing offices and the healthcare provider after analyzing all relevant patient data and assigning the appropriate codes for diagnosis, treatment, and billing.

You will have a variety of work locations to choose from if you are a qualified coder. Coders are employed by long-term care homes, insurance companies, hospitals, specialty clinics, and private physician offices. After gaining years of experience, one can start their own independent company that provides coding services to hospitals, physicians, and insurers.

The Responsibilities

A qualified professional coder supervises a medical facility's daily medical coding activities and makes sure that they adhere to all rules and regulations. Typically, their duties include providing facilities with code, maintaining databases, and conducting reviews and evaluations to spot errors or omissions and take corrective action. Additionally, it is crucial for a qualified professional coder to work with other parties like insurance companies and patients to coordinate with them, respond to their questions, and clarify procedures, as well as address any concerns they may have.

Many certified professional coders need to possess a specific set of abilities in order to carry out their duties. The most prevalent ones are analytical abilities, attention to detail, and integrity.

Here are some examples of responsibilities and tasks that you are likely to perform as a certified professional coder:

- Manage all aspects of medical office administration, A/P, A/R, medical billing, coordinate surgeries/deliveries, and maintain physician credentials.

- Utilize ICD-10-CM, CPT-4 codes, and modifiers in accordance with federal regulations.

- Determine and assign all appropriate diagnosis, procedure, and E/M codes to IP/OP visit according to coding guidelines.

- Code reports in a variety of specialties including: physiciary, emergency room, radiology, anesthesia, and assistant surgeons.

- Verify diagnosis codes to make sure they are accurate, specific, and relevant in compliance with Medicare rules.

- Assign ICD-9-CM, CPT-4, and HCPC codes accurately and timely (Zippia, 2020b).

CHAPTER 1:

ABOUT THE TEST

1.1 Introduction to the CPC Exam

The CPC exam is a competency examination for medical coding composed of 100 multiple-choice questions evaluating 17 subject categories. The majority of the questions include a coding scenario to evaluate how well medical professionals have used ICD-10-CM diagnostic codes, HCPCS Level II supply codes, and CPT® procedure codes when submitting claims to payers. You will use the AMA's CPT® Professional Edition, as well as your choice of ICD-10-CM and HCPCS Level II code guides, as approved coding reference materials during the exam. To pass the CPC exam, you must finish it in four hours and accurately answer 70% of the questions. The last stage of obtaining CPC certification—recognized throughout the healthcare industry as the gold standard for physician-based medical coding—is the Certified Professional Coder (CPC) exam.

You can become a healthcare business professional known for credible mastery of professional-fee medical coding by passing the CPC exam and obtaining the privilege to add the CPC abbreviation to your name (AAPC, 2019).

In light of the COVID-19 pandemic, the AAPC now offers a new CPC online exam consisting of two parts that will be available on Blackboard in two separate sessions and proctored by Examity®. On the day of each exam session, you will connect with your proctor through Examity, via Blackboard, to complete the authentication process and take the exam. Results will be posted 3–5 business days after your final exam session is complete. You will need a reliable Internet connection and an external webcam that can be positioned to show your face, hands, keyboard, and the area surrounding your keyboard, about 10 inches. Make sure that your location is quiet and private so that you're not disturbed (AAPC, 2019).

1.2 The Structure of the Exam

You must correctly answer a minimum of 70 questions from the series below in order to pass the CPC exam. However, the exam questions won't be labeled or organized according to the series to which they apply. A level of understanding that enables you to recognize the series will be required to complete the test.

10,000 Series CPT®

Six questions pertaining to surgical procedures carried out on the integumentary system make up the 10,000 Series CPT® portion of the exam. This comprises nails, pilonidal cysts, repairs, destruction, and the breast, along with skin, subcutaneous, and accessory structures (AAPC, 2019).

20,000 Series CPT®

The six questions in the 20,000 Series CPT® will focus on surgical techniques used to treat the entire musculoskeletal system. The head, neck, back and flank, spine, abdomen, shoulder, arm, hand and fingers, pelvis and hip, leg, foot, and toes are specifically addressed here (AAPC, 2019).

30,000 Series CPT®

Surgical procedures performed on the respiratory system, cardiovascular system, hemic and lymphatic systems, and the mediastinum and diaphragm are the subjects of six questions covering the 30,000 Series CPT® (AAPC, 2019).

40,000 Series CPT®

Six questions pertaining to surgical procedures performed on the digestive system will test your understanding of the 40,000 Series CPT®. These questions will consist of the following areas: esophagus, stomach, intestines, appendix, rectum, anus, liver, biliary tract, pancreas, abdomen, peritoneum, and omentum (AAPC, 2019).

50,000 Series CPT®

Six questions on surgical procedures performed on the urinary system, the male reproductive system; the female reproductive system, including maternity and delivery, and the endocrine system will be included in the CPC exam to test your knowledge of the 50,000 Series CPT® (AAPC, 2019).

60,000 Series CPT®

The 60,000 Series CPT® will include six questions that cover surgical procedures administered to the nervous system and include codes for the skull, meninges, brain, spine, spinal cord, extracranial nerves, peripheral nerves, and autonomic nervous system (AAPC, 2019).

Evaluation and Management

Your coding knowledge will be evaluated using six E/M questions that relate to the location and level of services, including office/other outpatients, hospital observation, hospital inpatient, consultations, emergency department, critical care, nursing facility, domiciliary and rest homes, and home services. Preventive medicine, non-face-to-face services, neonatal and pediatric critical care, intensive care, extended services, chronic care, transitional care, case management, and care plan supervision will all be addressed in the exam (AAPC, 2019).

Anesthesia

There will be four anesthesia-related questions, covering time reporting, qualifying circumstances, physical status modifiers, and anesthetic for surgical, diagnostic, and obstetric treatments (AAPC, 2019).

> What will be included in the exam from the 50,000 Series CPT® ?

Radiology

This area of the CPC exam will have six questions on diagnostic and interventional radiology, such as diagnostic ultrasound, radiologic guidance, mammography, bone, and joint studies, radiation oncology, and nuclear medicine (AAPC, 2019).

Laboratory / Pathology

Your understanding of organ and disease panels, therapeutic drug assays, drug testing, evocation/suppression testing, consultations, urinalysis, molecular pathology, MAAA chemistry, hematology and coagulation, immunology, transfusions, microbiology, anatomic pathology, cytopathology, cytogenetic studies, surgical pathology, in vivo and reproductive will be assessed by six path/lab questions (AAPC, 2019).

Medicine

Six questions will cover a variety of specialty-specific coding scenarios, including vaccinations, biofeedback, dialysis, central nervous system assessments, health and behavior assessments, hydration, medical nutrition, therapeutic and diagnostic administration, chemotherapy administration, photodynamic therapy, osteopathic manipulative treatment, patient education and training, non-face-to-face non-physician services, and moderate sedation (AAPC, 2019).

Medical Terminology

Four questions will evaluate your knowledge of medical terminology for all human bodily systems (AAPC, 2019).

Anatomy

Four questions will be used to evaluate each system's anatomy in the human body (AAPC, 2019).

ICD-10-CM/Diagnosis

Five questions will require expertise in diagnosis for the ICD-10-CM chapters as well as an excellent understanding of the ICD-10-CM Official Guidelines for Coding and Reporting. Additionally, other exam areas will include diagnosis questions from the CPT® categories (AAPC, 2019).

HCPCS Level II

There will be three HCPCS Level II coding-related questions on the CPC exam, covering topics like modifiers, supplies, medicines, and professional services for Medicare patients (AAPC, 2019).

Coding Guidelines

The ICD-10-CM Official Guidelines for Coding and Reporting, the CPT® coding guidelines and parenthetical notes, and the use of modifiers will all be covered in seven questions in this area of the CPC exam (AAPC, 2019).

Compliance and Regulatory

> **What will be covered in the HCPCS level II part of the exam?**

You will be asked three questions about applying coding to payment policies, place of service reporting, fraud, and abuse, National Correct Coding Initiative (NCCI) edits, national coverage determination/local coverage determination (NCD/LCD), Health Insurance Portability and Accountability Act (HIPAA), Advance Beneficiary Notices (ABNs), and Relative Value Units (RVUs), which are all related to services covered by Medicare Parts A, B, C, and D (AAPC, 2019).

Case (New Section)

You will be put to the test on your ability to correctly code medical record documentation using CPT®, ICD-10-CM, and HCPCS Level II using ten cases and one multiple-choice question per case. The 10,000, 20,000, 30,000, 40,000, 50,000, and 60,000 series will be covered. As well as, pathology, laboratory, radiology, medicine, anesthesia, and evaluation and management services. The cases may also test your knowledge of medical terminology, anatomy, compliance, and regulatory information (AAPC, 2019).

1.3 Exam Scoring

You need to get 105 of the 150 questions on the CPC exam right in order to pass. If you answered 105 out of 150 questions correctly, you may get all ten E/M questions incorrect and still pass the test as a whole. Therefore, it's possible for you to answer 45 questions incorrectly. For example, you would have a % average if you received 65% in one section and 75% in another (Hulme, 2021). The important thing to remember is that this exam is not testing your memory; it's testing your ability to find the best answer in any given situation.

1.4 Test-Taking Tips

General Preparation

Because the CPC exam includes so many topics, it is easy to become overwhelmed during the study process. You'll spend the majority of the exam referring to the CPT manual. Focusing your study efforts on the CPT code set is a good idea since there are far more questions that pertain to it than there are questions on ICD-10-CM codes and HCPCS. Know the manual inside and out, and be confident utilizing all of its appendices. Most people wait until they've worked in coding for a while before taking the exam (for the CPC, a passing grade and two years of professional experience—or the educational equivalent—are necessary for certification.). If you've gained that experience, you should have working knowledge of anatomy and physiology. But it's still a good idea to revisit this material using flashcards or study guides. Although certain exam questions will clearly reference medical or anatomical terms, possessing a solid medical vocabulary will also help you understand other questions (Medical Billing and Coding, 2022).

After you've done your studying, make sure to use as many practice exams as you can get your hands on. Treat these tests as if they were actual tests by studying hard for them, keeping track of your time while you take them, and then making note of the questions—and more importantly, the types of questions—that you consistently get incorrect. Did you have trouble with the anesthetic codes on your first test? Review that part one more time. Did you use incorrect ICD-10-CM codes? Examine the ICD-10-CM guide. Many private businesses provide CPC practice examinations but the AAPCs are probably your best option. Practice tests shouldn't be viewed as time wasters or formalities. Even though many practice examinations are simpler than the real thing, you should still treat them seriously. Before taking the actual CPC exam, you should attempt to achieve a score of at least 80% on a practice test (Medical Billing and Coding, 2022).

Before the Exam

When you have a goal, having a vision for the future helps. A plan makes decisions on spur-of-the-moment distractions in advance. A plan organizes assistance, avoiding stress and uncertainty. When the going becomes difficult, a plan tallies the costs, removing elements of surprise. Your plan does not need to be finalized, only anticipated. Create a mental picture of what it will take to get you to the finish line. And make a commitment (AAPC, 2021).

- **It should be a top priority to pass the test.** Create a plan that tackles your weaknesses. Maybe you have to avoid using your phone or TV until you've completed your day's worth of studying. Perhaps doing so means joining a study group. Don't wait too long between studying sessions.

> With the number of topics to study about,
> how will you go about studying each?

- **Take some time to focus.** As long as you're fully there and attentive, long study periods are fine. If you have a busy schedule or find it difficult to find a long period of time when you won't be tired, choose quality. Consider scheduling 15-minute study periods all day long. Find a schedule you can call your own by experimenting.

- **Believe fiercely.** You will have times of confusion, so be aware of this in advance. Keep your faith; it will pass. Trust in yourself: "I'm up to the task. I'll work hard because I deserve it." Your firewall is your belief. You must be confident that you can pass the test.

Keep in mind that not every subject in the CPC curriculum demands an equal amount of study time as you are preparing. You might recall from your CPC training course that some chapters require more time to process than others. For instance, evaluation and management are more difficult than the chapter on the urinary system. The same difficulties will have an impact on how you allocate your study time. Pay attention to the more complicated parts. Spend the time and effort necessary to fully comprehend important ideas and challenging situations. HIV, metastatic cancer, chronic pain, and infusions are a few examples. Identify your areas of weakness and focus more on them (AAPC, 2021).

Your modifiers, medical terminology, the letter ranges for the ICD-10-CM, and the numerical ranges for CPT® codes are the top three things you have to know. Understand the basic principles involved in applying each modifier and when to do so. You'll need to be familiar with anatomy and medical terminology in order to extract crucial information for coding. Get used to the language used in the code books. Code descriptors and code notes are used in exam questions. To search for the answers, you'll need to grasp the language clearly (AAPC, 2021).

Bring out the flashcards to review for the test. Being able to recognize a code's fundamental characteristics because you are familiar with its ranges can make the difference between passing the CPC exam and running out of time on test day.

Know the Official Code Guidelines

The guidelines give advice on how to choose a good code. Coders must thoroughly read their code books and pay close attention to the guidelines. Review each code set's guidelines, frequently, paying special attention to the more difficult ones. The objective is to understand the rules rather than to remember them. Understanding how to analyze and apply what you read is essential. By the day of the exam, you should be able to understand the rationale, purpose, logic, and intent of the guidelines (AAPC, 2021). Review the codes that the guideline relates to in order to determine how to apply it. Also practice!

Learn the fundamental applications. Make certain that you can respond correctly to 'Includes', 'Excludes', 'Code First', 'Code Also', and so on. Check your ability to follow sequencing guidelines. This is significantly weighted in the CPC exam (as in real-world coding). You should practice sequencing. Know where to look for specific guidelines as well as what themes are covered in chapter-specific guidelines. You don't have to remember where each guideline is; all you have to do is tab and mark your books. Furthermore, chapter-specific guidelines will inform you when you should verify a guideline before making a code decision. Remember to go over coding conventions and notations, excluding notes for ICD-10, as well as parenthetical notes for CPT® (AAPC, 2021).

Prep Your Medical Code Books

Everything you need to know for the CPC exam is in your CPT®, ICD-10-CM, and HCPCS Level II coding books. The better you know your books, the easier exam day will be for you. The goal is to be able to rapidly access anything and everything—codes, guidelines, tables, instructions, illustrations, and so on—so keep familiarizing yourself with the different sections of your books (AAPC, 2021).

It would be a good idea to tab your books. Most people reserve tabbing for guidelines and chapters in tabular lists but you can tab anything you need extra help with. You could also wish to tab items that you don't regularly look for. These are your books, so label and mark them accordingly (AAPC, 2021). Some people believe tabs are inconvenient, while others believe they are necessary for the exam. Follow your instincts.

When marking your books, be strategic. You don't want to lose essential notes amid the clutter of too many notes. The same is true with highlighted text. Keep your notations as relevant to the exam as possible. Make notes and keep them somewhere you can locate them easily. Some people would rather write small notes around the codes than fill blank pages with notes. Choose whatever method helps you find what you're looking for quickly. You are not permitted to add writing surfaces to your books. It is not permitted to tape, glue, or staple anything into your code books. Sticky notes are included in this (AAPC, 2021).

When making notes in your books for codes that have guidelines that give you problems, write the guideline next to the code. Some people do the opposite, putting code examples next to the guideline. You could also create an E/M table to assist you in determining E/M services (CPT®) and label the sequence codes (CPT®). Write procedure definitions next to CPT codes, or use subtle variations of body parts or layers to highlight differences across codes (e.g., integumentary). It also helps to write key phrases, prefixes, and suffixes next to appropriate body parts on your anatomical illustration pages (AAPC, 2021). Only use the methods that you find helpful.

Highlight code first notes, use additional code notes, and mark codes that are excluded from a category in ICD-10. Highlight keywords in subsection guidelines (for example, new and established patient definition in the E/M section); keywords in the Repair (Closure) guideline section defining simple, intermediate, or complex repairs; and keywords in the Musculoskeletal System guidelines defining surgical procedures such as closed, opened, percutaneous skeletal fixation, or manipulation in the CPT®. Make a note of any guidelines for Adjacent Tissue Transfer or Rearrangement procedures, as well as all parenthetical notes listed in the code description or following the code, and procedures conducted percutaneously, with any sort of scope (endoscope, laparoscope, etc.), or by open method (meaning the physician had to cut into the patient to perform the procedure) also in the CPT® (AAPC, 2021).

After you've studied, you'll want to take as many practice examinations as possible. As previously said, treat the practice tests as if they were the actual thing. Return to the areas where you struggled. Retest and repeat. Continue to work on your time management, test-taking abilities, and accuracy. To finish the CPC exam in the four hours allocated, you must answer questions in 2.4 minutes or less. To improve your speed, practice like an athlete. Also, practice crossing out answers using what you've learned. Answer elimination is a good method for both accuracy and time management. And keep practicing until you get a minimum of 80% (AAPC, 2021).

Exam Day

The Day Before

Read your guidelines three days before the exam so that they are fresh in your mind during the week of your exam. Check the start time and examination location a few days before your test date. If you are unfamiliar with the exam location, consider pre-planning your driving routes. Allow for unexpected delays along the way and arrive 10–15 minutes early. Make sure you have everything you need for the exam: code books, a printed copy of the ICD-10-CM Official Guidelines, a surplus of #2 pencils, an eraser, a photo ID, and a member ID. It's also a good idea to bring a watch or stopwatch with you to keep track of time (AAPC, 2021).

Note: On the printed side of the ICD-10-CM Official Guidelines, you may highlight, underline, and make brief notations. Long lengths of content are not permitted on the printout's blank pages. Smartwatches and other internet-connected devices are also prohibited. If you haven't previously, confirm what exam materials are permitted for the CPC exam.

Additionally, if you're taking the CPC exam online, make sure your camera is up to snuff. It's never a bad idea to have a backup plan in case of unexpected technical issues. (The materials permitted for the online exam differ from those permitted for the onsite exam, so confirm which resources are accepted. A printed copy of the ICD-10-CM Official Guidelines, for example, is not permitted (AAPC, 2021)).

The day before the exam, close your books. You're done studying. If you're taking the test online, check your webcam and set up your test area before getting a good night's rest. Enjoy a good meal (nothing too heavy) in the morning, and bring small snacks and water to keep you energized during the exam (AAPC, 2021). Maintain a positive attitude. Breathe. Recite your mantra: "I can do this. I've got this." Slow, deep breaths. You are ready. You've worked hard to get here.

The Day Of

Before the exam begins, pay close attention while the proctor reads the instructions. If you don't understand something, ask questions. And request a last call. Whether you brought a watch or not, it's a good idea to ask your proctor to call time when 15 minutes are left. This heads-up will allow you to go back and fill in any questions you've left blank. As previously said, four hours provide you with approximately two minutes and 40 seconds to answer each question. If you keep a 2-minute pace and don't get delayed on too many questions, you'll be able to answer all 100 questions without having to make a last-minute dash. Keep a close watch on the time. Set a non-smart wristwatch or stopwatch to vibrate in two-minute intervals if you brought one. This will tell you how much time you've spent on a question and prompt you to move on if you've gone over the two-minute limit (AAPC, 2022).

When you begin the exam, start with the simple anatomy questions at the back of the test booklet and work your way forward from there. These simple questions are brief but contribute equally to your overall score. By tackling them first, you'll have more time to answer them all and will be able to concentrate on the case study questions with a better feeling of time remaining and less pressure. And before reading the extensive operative report attached to the question, read the question. Sometimes a question will apply to only a small portion of the report, such as date of service discrepancy, and noting this beforehand will save you a lot of time (AAPC, 2022).

Additionally, highlight keywords in the test booklet to assist you in looking up the code. Take note of words like not, except, most, least, and greatest, as these are frequently crucial in determining the correct answer. You should also omit everything in the case report that isn't relevant to the question. This could assist you in eliminating answers. Remember that code notes are used to define terms, clarify information, or list choices for additional characters. When checking codes, pay close attention to them as they contain essential information and can help you avoid mistakes (AAPC, 2022).

Also, avoid second-guessing yourself. Go through a question as quickly as possible and rely on your first educated response. The last thing you want to do is get caught up in overthinking. Keep in mind that keeping up the pace means answering more exam questions, which equals a higher score. Make a logical deduction and move on if you are stuck on a difficult question. You can return to the question later if you have time. You don't want to spend so much time answering one question that you can't answer any others. Make a mental note of difficult questions and return to them later. Caution: If you skip a question in the test booklet, make sure you skip the question on the grid as well so your answers line up properly. (This is where having a ruler comes in handy.) And never ever leave a question unanswered. While leaving an answer blank is definitely incorrect, taking a guess might just give you the right answer. But save your guessing for the last 15–20 minutes of the CPC exam, when you have no other choice (AAPC, 2022).

You can't check every code in all four multiple-choice answers due to time constraints. You'll need to employ a calculated strategy and rule out as many options as you can. You just need to verify which of the two remaining options is true if you can eliminate two. How would you employ the method of elimination? To assist you in deciding on two answers, read the question again before scanning the case for important words. Does the code's first character correspond to the right code range? For instance, if a question relates to the musculoskeletal system, you can exclude all CPT® codes that don't start with two (AAPC, 2022).

Check sequencing. Do secondary codes appear on the list of primary codes? If so, disregard this answer. Can you eliminate a response using EXCLUDES notes or other exemptions? What about an improper modifier? See the notes next to the codes. Based on note details, you may frequently rule out answers. Do two answers mention a code? If so, immediately check that code to see if it matches the op notes, and, based on what you discover, eliminate two answers. The guidelines for the CPT® and ICD-10-CM codes in the remaining answers must only be checked if you can eliminate two choices, putting you halfway to the right answer. Check to see if you've answered all the questions using the remaining exam time. Review your best guesses if you still have time to see if you can come up with a more reliable answer (AAPC, 2022).

Some general advice:

- Bring earplugs. Large, otherwise silent, rooms amplify sounds like chairs sliding against the floor or throat clearing. Be ready to minimize sounds from detracting from your focus.

- Bring some snacks. You should pick food that you can get and eat quietly. Consider cheese in contrast to crisp celery or chips packaged in crinkly paper.

- You can use a ruler to keep track of the rows on the answer page and make sure you fill in the correct row.

- Avoid being distracted. Don't let other people finishing early worry you. As they say, keep calm and carry on. Utilize all of the time at your disposal.

Formative Assessment Questions:

1. How is the CPC exam structured?
2. Why should you prepare your coding books?
3. How is the CPC exam scored?
4. What are the top three things to remember before the exam?

Key Concepts

- The **CPC exam** is a competency examination for medical coding composed of 100 multiple-choice questions evaluating 17 subject categories.

- Most of the questions include a coding scenario to evaluate how well medical professionals have used **ICD-10-CM diagnostic codes, HCPCS Level II supply codes, and CPT® procedure codes** when submitting claims to payers

- Structure of the exam is as follows:

  - **10,000 Series CPT®**: six questions about the surgical procedures on the integumentary system

  - **20,000 Series CPT®**: six questions about the surgical procedures on the musculoskeletal system

  - **30,000 Series CPT®**: six questions about the surgical procedures on the respiratory, cardiovascular, hemic, and lymphatic systems

  - **40,000 Series CPT®**: six questions about the surgical procedures on the digestive system

  - **50,000 Series CPT®**: six questions about the surgical procedures on the urinary system, male and the female reproductive system, and endocrine system

  - **60,000 Series CPT®**: six questions about the surgical procedures on the nervous system

  - **Evaluation and Management**: six questions

- **Anesthesia**: four questions

- **Radiology**: six questions

- **Laboratory/Pathology**: six questions

- **Medicine**: six questions

- **Medical terminology**: four questions

- **Anatomy**: Four questions

- **ICD-10-CM/Diagnosis**: Five questions

- **HCPCS Level II**: three questions

- **Coding Guidelines**: seven questions

- **Compliance and Regulatory**: three questions

- **Case**: ten cases, one multiple-choice questions

You need to get **105 of the 150 questions** on the CPC exam right in order to pass.

CHAPTER 2:

CURRENT PROCEDURAL TERMINOLOGY (CPT) SURGICAL PROCEDURES

2.1 Integumentary System: 10030–19499

Skin, nails, hair, sebaceous and sudoriferous glands, and the breast all belong to the integumentary system. The skin serves as a covering to safeguard other body parts. The skin has a crucial role in controlling body temperature and serves as the touch-sensing organ. Through the skin, vitamin D, which is vital for strong bones, is absorbed. Since the skin serves as the body's first line of defense, it frequently sustains damage. The Integumentary System uses numerous CPT codes to document the treatments for wounds, burns, ulcers, and unusual skin growths. Sometimes more involved treatments are needed to heal damaged skin, such as grafts, adjacent tissue transfers, or the application of skin replacement therapies (Bernard et al., 2015).

The six integumentary components of toenails and fingernails are the nail root, bed, nail plate, eponychium (cuticle), perionychium, and hyponychium. At the proximal nail, the nail root (germinal matrix) is located beneath the skin. This is where new nails are formed. The nail bed is the vascular tissue right below the nail plate, and the nail plate is the portion of the nail that is visible from the cuticle to the tip of the finger. At the base of the nail plate, the eponychium serves as a seal, while the perionychium serves as the skin barrier at the sides of the nail bed. The intersection of the fingertip and the distal edge nail plate is known as the hyponychium (Bernard et al., 2015).

The integumentary system includes the female breast. With a network of ducts connecting the lobules, where milk is produced during lactation, to the nipple, where the milk is released, it is mostly made of adipose tissue. The Cooper suspensory ligaments hold the breast in place over the pectoralis major muscle between the second and sixth ribs. Ptosis results from the long-term stretching of these ligaments. The areola, which has lubricating sebaceous glands, is where the nipple is located. The tail of Spence, or adipose breast tissue, spreads into the armpit. More complicated structures like the chest wall, ribs, or pectoral muscles may be affected by procedures on the breast. Breast cancer-related excision and biopsy CPT codes do not differentiate between sexes (Bernard et al., 2015).

Skin, Subcutaneous, and Accessory Structures: 10030 – 11646

Introduction and Removal

Catheter drainage allows fluid from the body to drain into a collection device. Image guidance may be required in some cases to access the site to be drained. Code 10030 is reported once for each individual catheter placed in soft tissue using image guidance, excluding peritoneal, retroperitoneal, transvaginal, transrectal, and visceral collections (Bernard et al., 2015).

10030: Drainage of image-guided fluid collections via catheter (e.g., abscess, hematoma, seroma, lymphocele, cyst), soft tissue (e.g., extremity, abdominal wall, neck), percutaneous (Bernard et al., 2015)

Incision and Drainage

Integumentary incision and drainage (I&D) is a procedure used to drain purulent or pressurized fluids from beneath or within the skin. The goal of I&D procedures is incision rather than excision. These codes denote procedures in which the doctor uses methods including cavity exploration, swabbing, lavage, and irrigation to actively drain the incised site. Foreign bodies are also extracted from the skin or subcutaneous tissue using I&D. Integumentary codes for I&D are assigned based on the type of defect (e.g., foreign body, pilonidal cyst, abscess, hematoma) and whether the procedure was complicated (Bernard et al., 2015).

10040: Acne surgery (e.g., marsupialization)

10060: Abscess incision and drainage (e.g., cutaneous or subcutaneous abscess); simple or single

10061: complicated or multiple

10080: Simple incision and drainage of pilonidal cyst

10081: complicated

10120: Simple incision and removal of foreign body, subcutaneous tissues

10121: complicated

10140: Hematoma, seroma, or fluid collection incision and drainage

10160: Abscess, hematoma, bulla, or cyst aspiration via puncture

10180: Incision and drainage, complicated, postoperative wound infection (Bernard et al., 2015)

Debridement

Debridement is the process of removing contaminated or damaged tissue. CPT codes 11000–11047 are used to document wound debridement to depths involving subcutaneous tissue, muscle or fascia, and bone. CPT codes 97597 and 97598 are used to report epidermis and dermis debridement. The debridement depth reported is the deepest depth of tissue removed. Only measure the area that will be debrided when determining body surface. Codes 16020–16030 are used to report burn debridement. The distinction between debridement and excision is that excision necessitates closure. Unless the debridement is related to a repair, which is the primary goal of the encounter, the debridement site is not closed (Bernard et al., 2015).

11000: Debridement of eczematous or infected skin on up to 10% of the body surface

11001: each additional 10% of the body surface, or a portion of it (should be listed separately in addition to the primary procedure code)

11004: Skin, subcutaneous tissue, muscle, and fascia debridement for necrotizing soft tissue infection; external genitalia and perineum

11005: with or without closure of the abdominal wall

11006: with or without fascial closure of the external genitalia, perineum, and abdominal wall

11008: Removal of prosthetic material or mesh, abdominal wall for infection (e.g., for chronic or recurring mesh infection) (List separately in addition to primary procedure code)

11010: Debridement includes the removal of foreign material from the site of an open fracture and/or dislocation (e.g. excisional debridement); skin and subcutaneous tissues.

11011: skin, subcutaneous tissue, muscle fascia, and muscle

11012: skin, subcutaneous tissue, muscle fascia, muscle, and bone

11042: Debridement of subcutaneous tissue (including epidermis and dermis when performed); first 20 sq cm or less

11045: each additional 20 sq cm, or portion thereof. List separately in addition to the code for the primary procedure

11043: Debridement, muscle, and/or fascia (including, if performed, epidermis, dermis, and subcutaneous tissue); first 20 sq cm or less

11046: each additional 20 sq cm, or portion thereof. List separately in addition to the code for the primary procedure

11044: Debridement of bone (includes epidermis, dermis, subcutaneous tissue, muscle, and/or fascia when performed); first 20 sq cm or less

11047: each additional 20 sq cm, or portion thereof. List separately in addition to the code for the primary procedure (Bernard et al., 2015)

Paring and Cutting

The integumentary system is made up of three layers: the epidermis, dermis, and subcutaneous tissue or hypodermis. The epidermis is formed in its innermost layer and becomes flatter and drier as it matures and reaches the skin's surface. Dead cells that have been shed and are being replaced every two weeks make up the top layer of the epidermis. The dermis is a complex layer made up of nerves, blood vessels, hair follicles, and glands. Hyperkeratotic lesions are thickened skin formed by epidermal expansion in order to protect the skin from local irritation (corns and calluses), inflammation (chronic eczema), and other immune system reactions. Codes 11055–11057 are used to report procedures that rarely require local anesthesia or chemical cauterization. Only one code should be reported based on the number of lesions treated during the encounter (Bernard et al., 2015).

11055: Single lesion cutting or paring of a benign hyperkeratotic lesion (such as a corn or callus)

11056: 2–4 lesions

11057: more than 4 lesions (Bernard et al., 2015)

Biopsy

A skin biopsy code's purpose is to describe a diagnostic technique in which the excised tissue goes through a separately reported pathological evaluation. The biopsy service is provided when skin is collected for biopsy as part of a broader surgical procedure. This range of codes is used to report biopsy and simple closure of the dermis, epidermis, or mucous membrane (Bernard et al., 2015).

11100: Unless otherwise specified, skin, subcutaneous tissue, and/or mucous membrane biopsy (including simple closure); only one lesion

11101: for each separate/additional lesion (should be listed separately in addition to the code for the primary procedures) (Bernard et al., 2015)

Removal of Skin Tags

A skin tag, also known as an acrochordon, is a fleshy dermal stalk that forms on the skin, particularly in areas where the skin creases, such as the neck, axilla, groin, and eyelid. Clothing or shaving may irritate these tags on a regular basis. CPT codes 11200 and 11201 are used to report skin tag removal by any method. Codes 46220 and 46230 are used to report the excision of anal tags as a result of hemorrhoids (Bernard et al., 2015).

11200: Removal of skin tags, multiple fibrocutaneous tags on any bodily area; up to and including 15 lesions

11201: each additional 10 lesions, or portion thereof (List in addition to code for primary procedure) (Bernard et al., 2015)

Shaving of Epidermal or Dermal Lesions

Shaving can be used to remove benign lesions that are completely contained within the dermis and epidermis. To undercut the lesion, the scalpel is held parallel to the skin while shaving. Traditional excisions involve holding the scalpel perpendicular to the skin and cutting the skin's edges before undermining the tissue to be removed. The wound that remains after shaving a lesion does not need to be closed (Bernard et al., 2015).

11300: Epidermal or dermal lesion shaving, single lesion, trunk, arms, or legs; lesion diameter of 0.5 cm or less

11301: lesion diameter 0.6–1.0 cm

11302: lesion diameter 1.1-2.0 cm

11303: lesions diameter over 2.0 cm

11305: Epidermal or dermal lesion shaving, single lesion, trunk, arms, or legs; lesion diameter of 0.5 cm or less

11306: lesion diameter 0.6–1.0 cm

11307: lesion diameter 1.1–2.0 cm

11308: lesions diameter over 2.0 cm

11310: Shaving a single epidermal or dermal lesion on the face, ears, eyelids, nose, lips, or mucous membrane; lesion diameter of 0.5 cm or less

11311: lesion diameter 0.6–1.0 cm

11312: lesion diameter 1.1–2.0 cm

11313: lesions diameter over 2.0 cm (Bernard et al., 2015)

Excision — Benign Lesions

Benign lesions are contained, which means they cannot invade neighboring tissues or metastasize. Lipomas, cysts, fibromas, nevi, and some moles are examples of benign skin lesions. This series of codes is used to report the excision of benign lesions that originate in the integumentary system. The lesion and excision may surpass the integumentary system. The benign lesion is usually excised with a margin of healthy full-thickness skin. The measurement required for CPT code selection is the diameter of the entire excision (including the margin). Any surgical site repair that necessitates layered closure, extensive undermining, or retention sutures should be reported separately. When a lesion's morphology is ambiguous, the coder should select rather than the final pathology report, the excision code categorization (malignant versus benign) is based on the physician's approach to the lesion. In this manner, regardless of the pathology report, the physician's knowledge, expertise, time, and effort will be reflected in the coding. A lesion suspected of being benign, for example, would be excised with smaller margins than a lesion suspected of being malignant (Bernard et al., 2015).

11400: Excision of benign lesions, including margins, except skin tags (unless otherwise specified), from the trunk, arms, or legs; excised diameter of 0.5 cm or less

11401: excised diameter 0.6–1.0 cm

11402: excised diameter 1.1–2.0 cm

11403: excised diameter 2.1–3.0 cm

11404: excised diameter 3.1–4.0 cm

11406: excised diameter over 4.0 cm

11420: Excision of benign lesions, including margins, excluding skin tags (unless otherwise specified), scalp, neck, hands, feet, and genitalia; excised diameter of 0.5 cm or less

11421: excised diameter 0.6–1.0 cm

11422: excised diameter 1.1–2.0 cm

11423: excised diameter 2.1–3.0 cm

11424: excised diameter 3.1–4.0 cm

11426: excised diameter over 4.0 cm

11440: Excision of other benign lesions, including margins, except skin tags (unless otherwise specified), from the face, ears, eyelids, nose, lips, and mucous membrane; excised diameter of 0.5 cm or less.

11441: excised diameter 0.6–1.0 cm

11442: excised diameter 1.1–2.0 cm

11443: excised diameter 2.1–3.0 cm

11444: excised diameter 3.1–4.0 cm

11446: excised diameter over 4.0 cm

11450: Excision of skin and subcutaneous tissue for axillary hidradenitis with simple or intermediate repair

11451: with complex repair

11462: Excision of skin and subcutaneous tissue for inguinal hidradenitis with simple or intermediate repair

11463: with complex repair

What is the code range of epidermal or dermal lesion shaving?

11470: Skin and subcutaneous tissue excision for hidradenitis, perianal, perineal, or umbilical; simple or intermediate repair

11471: with complex repair (Bernard et al., 2015)

Excision — Malignant Lesions

Malignant lesions have the potential to infiltrate or spread to surrounding tissues. Melanoma, basal cell, squamous cell, Merkel cell carcinoma, and Kaposi sarcoma are examples of malignant skin neoplasms. The CPT codes in this series are used to report the excision of cutaneous malignant lesions in the integumentary system. Malignancy and excision may spread beyond the integumentary system. The malignant lesion is removed with a large margin of healthy full-thickness skin or other surrounding tissue. Any surgical site repair that necessitates multilayer closure, significant undermining, retention sutures, or flaps and grafts should be documented separately (Bernard et al., 2015).

11600: Malignant lesion excision, involving margins, trunk, arms, or legs; excised diameter of 0.5 cm or less

11601:   excised diameter 0.6–1.0 cm

11602:   excised diameter 1.1–2.0 cm

11603:   excised diameter 2.1–3.0 cm

11604:   excised diameter 3.1–4.0 cm

11606: excised diameter greater than 4.0 cm

11620: Excision of a malignant lesion, comprising the margins, scalp, neck, hands, feet, and genitalia; excised diameter of 0.5 cm or less

11621:   excised diameter 0.6–1.0 cm

11622:   excised diameter 1.1–2.0 cm

11623:   excised diameter 2.1–3.0 cm

11624:   excised diameter 3.1–4.0 cm

11626:   excised diameter greater than 4.0 cm

11640: Malignant lesion excision, including margins, face, ears, eyelids, nose, and lips; excised diameter 0.5 cm or less

11641: excised diameter 0.6–1.0 cm

11642: excised diameter 1.1–2.0 cm

11643: excised diameter 2.1–3.0 cm

11644: excised diameter 3.1–4.0 cm

11646: excised diameter greater than 4.0 cm (Bernard et al., 2015)

Nails: 11719–11765

Debridement can be used to treat hypertrophic, mycotic, or dystrophic nails. The physician utilizes instruments (such as nail splitters, elevators, or electrical burrs) to remove extraneous tissue from the nail during debridement. Chronic onychocryptosis, often known as an ingrown toenail, occurs when the nail grows into the perionychium, or skin on the side of the nail bed. This can result in chronic pain and infection and can be treated surgically, with laser, electrocautery, or chemical procedures that destroy or remove all or part of the nail and nail matrix. The removal or destruction of the matrix assures that the corresponding nail does not regrow (Bernard et al., 2015).

11719: Trimming of any number of nondystrophic nails

11720: Debridement of nail(s) by any method(s); 1–5

11721: 6 or more

11730: Partial or complete avulsion of nail plate, simple; single

11732: each additional nail plate should be listed separately in addition to the code for the primary procedure

11740: Evacuation of subungual hematoma

11750: Partial or complete excision of the nail and nail matrix (e.g., ingrown or deformed nail), for permanent removal

11752: with amputation of tuft of distal phalanx

11755: Biopsy of the nail unit, such as plate, bed, matrix, hyponychium, proximal, and lateral nail folds (separate procedure)

11760: Repair of nail bed

11762: Reconstruction of the nail bed with a graft

11765: Wedge excision of skin of the nail fold (e.g., for ingrown toenail) (Bernard et al., 2015)

Pilonidal Cyst: 11770–11772

When hair becomes trapped in the skin around the tailbone at the top of the buttock cleft, it creates a pilonidal cyst or sinus. Pilonidal cysts can get infected and recur. The codes 11770 – 11772 are used to report cyst excision (pilonidal cystectomy). CPT code selection is determined by the extent of the excision and whether the excision is complicated by infection or other problems, such as multiple fistulas. Report code 10080 or 10081 if an infected pilonidal cyst is treated solely with incision and drainage (I&D) (Bernard et al., 2015).

11770: Simple excision of pilonidal cyst or sinus

11771: extensive

11772: complicated (Bernard et al., 2015)

Introduction: 11900–11983

Codes 11900 and 11901 are used to report the treatment of integumentary lesions such as keloids, psoriasis, and acne with a therapeutic substance injected directly into the defect. Because a single lesion may be treated with many injections, code selection is based on the number of lesions treated rather than the number of injections. Codes 11900 and 11901 should not be recorded in the same report. Chemotherapeutic lesion injection is coded as 96405 or 96406 (Bernard et al., 2015).

11900: Intralesional injection of up to and including 7 lesions

11901: more than 7 lesions

11920: Tattooing, intradermal introduction of insoluble opaque pigments to correct color defects of skin, including micropigmentation; on 6.0 sq cm of the skin or less

11921:   6.1–20.0 sq cm

11922: each additional 20.0 sq cm, or portion thereof should be listed separately in addition to the code for the primary procedure

11950: Subcutaneous injection of a filling material (such as collagen); 1 cc or less

11951:   1.1–5.0 cc

11952:   5.1–10.0 cc

11954:   more than 10.0 cc

11960: Insertion of tissue expander(s) for area other than the breast, including subsequent expansion

11970: Replacement of a tissue expander with permanent prosthesis

11971: Removal of a tissue expander(s) without insertion of prosthesis

11976: Removal of implantable contraceptive capsules

11980: Subcutaneous hormone pellet implantation (pellets beneath the skin)

11981: Insertion of non-biodegradable drug delivery implant

11982: Removal of non-biodegradable drug delivery implant

11983: Removal with reinsertion of non-biodegradable drug delivery implant (Bernard et al., 2015)

Repair (Closure): 12001–16036

Repair — Simple

Integumentary repair codes are used to report skin closure operations that involve tissue adhesives, sutures, or staples in any combination or alone. A repair involving only adhesive strips should be documented using the appropriate E/M service code. A simple repair is reported for wound closure that is a single layer and does not have considerable wound contamination. Simple repair includes local anesthetic and cauterization (Bernard et al., 2015).

12001: Simple repair of open wounds of scalp, neck, axillae, external genitalia, trunk, and/or extremities (including hands and feet); 2.5 cm or less

12002:   2.6–7.5 cm

12004:   7.6–12.5 cm

12005: 12.6–20.0 cm

12006: 20.1–30.0 cm

12007: greater than 30.0 cm

12011: Simple repair of open wounds of the face, ears, eyelids, nose, lips, and/or mucous membranes; 2.5 cm or less

12013: 2.6–5.0 cm

12014: 5.1–7.5 cm

12015: 7.6–12.5 cm

12016: 12.6–20.0 cm

12017: 20.1–30.0 cm

12018: over 30.0 cm

12020: Treatment of superficial wound dehiscence; simple closure

12021: with packing (Bernard et al., 2015)

Repair — Intermediate

An intermediate repair is reported for wound closure with more than one layer or with a single layer but requiring significant cleaning. By merging the wound lengths documented, any identical wounds (simple, intermediate, or complicated) that are classified to the same anatomical grouping may be integrated into a single code (for example, for code 12036, intermediate wounds of the scalp, axillae, trunk, and extremities, except hands and feet) (Bernard et al., 2015).

12031: Intermediate repair of wounds of extremities (except hands and feet), trunk, axillae, and/or scalp; 2.5 cm or less

12032:   2.6–7.5 cm

12034:   7.6–12.5 cm

12035:   12.6–20.0 cm

12036:   20.1–30.0 cm

12037:   more than 30.0 cm

12041: Intermediate repair of wounds of neck, hands, feet, and/or external genitalia; 2.5 cm or less

12042:   2.6–7.5 cm

12044:   7.6–12.5 cm

12045:   12.6–20.0 cm

12046:   20.1–30.0 cm

12047:   over 30.0 cm

12051: Intermediate repair of wounds of the nose, lips, mucous membranes, face, ears, and/or eyelids; 2.5 cm or less

12052:   2.6–5.0 cm

12053:   5.1–7.5 cm

12054:   7.6–12.5 cm

12055:   12.6–20.o cm

12056:   20.1–30.o cm

12057:   over 30.0 cm (Bernard et al., 2015)

Repair — Complex

Complex repairs include layering the closure of deeper tissues such superficial fascia and subcutaneous tissue, debridement, extensive undermining, stents, and retention sutures. Any nerve, vascular, or tendon repair is documented separately. Any wound repair procedure includes simple wound investigation. Debridement is documented separately only when cleaning is extended or considerable volumes of tissue are removed during a complex repair (Bernard et al., 2015).

13100: Complex repair of trunk; 1.1–2.5 cm

13101:   2.6–7.5 cm

13102: each additional 5 cm or less should be listed separately in addition to the code for the primary procedure

13120: Complex repair of scalp, arms, and/or legs; 1.1–2.5 cm

13121:   2.6–7.5 cm

13122: each additional 5 cm or less should be listed separately in addition to the code for the primary procedure

13131: Complex repair of the forehead, cheeks, chin, mouth, neck, axillae, genitalia, hands and/or feet; 1.1–2.5 cm

13132:   2.6–7.5 cm

13133: each additional 5 cm or less should be listed separately in addition to the code for the primary procedure

13151: Complex repair of eyelids, nose, ears and/or lips; 1.1–2.5 cm

13152:   2.6–7.5 cm

13153: each additional 5 cm or less should be listed separately in addition to the code for the primary procedure

13160: The secondary closure of a surgical wound or dehiscence, extensive, or complicated (Bernard et al., 2015)

Adjacent tissue transfer or rearrangement

Skin undermining along with further skin incisions to hide a defect are reported as codes for nearby tissue transfer or rearrangement. In an adjacent tissue transfer or rearrangement, the skin is always attached to one or more of its borders. Codes are assigned based on the location and extent of the problem. When a lesion excision repair involves adjacent tissue transfer, the lesion excision is reported as part of the adjacent tissue transfer and is not reported separately. Flaps are different from adjacent tissue transfers in that they are transferred to a nonadjacent recipient site (Bernard et al., 2015).

14000: Adjacent tissue transfer or rearrangement of trunk; defect 10–30 sq cm or less

14001:   defect 10.1–30.0 sq cm

14020: Adjacent tissue transfer or rearrangement of the scalp, arms and/or legs; defect size of 10 sq cm or less

14021:   defect 10.1–30.0 sq cm

14040: Adjacent tissue transfer or rearrangement of forehead, cheeks, chin, mouth, neck, axillae, genitalia, hands and/or feet; defect 10 sq cm or less

14041:   defect 10.1–30.0 sq cm

14060: Adjacent tissue transfer or rearrangement of ears, eyelids, nose, and/or lips; defect size of 10 sq cm or less

14061:   defect 10.1–30.0 sq cm

14301: Adjacent tissue transfer or rearrangement of any area; defect 30.1–60.0 sq cm

14302: each additional 30.0 sq cm, or portion thereof. (list separately in addition to the code for the primary procedure)

14350: Fileted finger or toe flap, including the establishment of the recipient site (Bernard et al., 2015)

Skin replacement surgery

Skin replacement can be used to provide a permanent remedy to skin loss or injury, or it can be used to provide a temporary covering for a burn or non-healing lesion. For skin replacement, the following two coding components are required: surgical site preparation and graft material application. Skin grafts are essentially autotransplantations in which skin from one region of the body is removed and transplanted to another part of the same body. A full-thickness skin graft (FTSG) is made up of the entire epidermis and dermis. A split-thickness skin graft (STSG) is made up of the epidermis and a portion of the dermis. Skin substitutes or skin cultures can also be used to make grafts (Bernard et al., 2015).

Surgical Preparation

15002: Excision of open wounds, burn eschar, scars (including subcutaneous tissues), or incisional release of scar contracture, trunk, arms, and legs; first 100 sq cm or 1% of the body area of newborns and children

15003: every additional 100 sq cm, or portion thereof, or every additional 1% of a child's or infant's body area (list separately in addition to the primary procedure codes)

15004: Excision of open wounds, burn eschar, or scars (including subcutaneous tissues), or incisional release of scar contracture, face, scalp, eyelids, mouth, neck, ears, orbits, genitalia, hands, feet, and/

or numerous digits; first 100 sq cm or 1% of body area of newborns and children

15005: every additional 100 sq cm, or portion thereof, or every additional 1% of a child's or infant's body area (list separately in addition to the primary procedure codes) (Bernard et al., 2015)

Autografts/Tissue Cultured Autograft

15040: Harvest of skin for a tissue cultured skin autograft, with a size of 100 sq cm or less

15050: Single or multiple pinch graft to cover small ulcer, or other minimal open area (except on the face), up to defect size 2 cm diameter

15100: Split-thickness autograft of trunk, arms, legs; first 100 sq cm or less, or 1% of body area of infants and children (except 15050)

15101: each additional 100 sq cm, or each additional 1% of body area of infants and children, or portion thereof (List separately in addition to the code to the primary procedure)

15110: Epidermal autograft of trunk, arms, or legs; first 100 sq cm or less, or 1% of body area of infants and children

15111: each additional 100 square centimeters, each additional 1% of a child's or infant's body area, or any portion thereof (list separately in addition to primary procedure code)

15115: Epidermal autograft of orbits, ears, mouth, eyelids, neck, face, scalp, hands, feet, genitalia, and/or multiple digits; first 100 sq cm or less, or 1% of the body area of infants and children

15116: each additional 100 square centimeters, each additional 1% of a child's or infant's body area, or any portion thereof (list separately in addition to primary procedure code)

15120: Split-thickness autograft of the orbits, ears, mouth, eyelids, neck, face, scalp, hands, feet, genitalia, and/or multiple digits; the first 100 sq cm or less, or 1% of body area of infants and children (except 15050)

15121: each additional 100 square centimeters, each additional 1% of a child's or infant's body area, or any portion thereof (list separately in addition to primary procedure code)

15130: Dermal autograft of the trunk, arms, or legs; first 100 sq cm or less, or 1% of body area of infants and children

15131: each additional 100 square centimeters, each additional 1% of a child's or infant's body area, or any portion thereof (list separately in addition to primary procedure code)

15135: Dermal autograft of the feet, genitalia, face, scalp, ears, neck, eyelids, orbits, mouth, hands, and/or multiple digits; first 100 sq cm or less, or 1% of body area of newborns and children

15136: each additional 100 square centimeters, each additional 1% of a child's or infant's body area, or any portion thereof (list separately in addition to primary procedure code)

15150: Tissue cultured skin autograft of trunk, arms, and legs; first 25 sq cm or less

15151: additional 1–75 sq cm (list separately in addition to the code for the primary procedure)

15152: each additional 100 square centimeters, each additional 1% of a child's or infant's body area, or any portion thereof (list separately in addition to primary procedure code)

15155: Tissue cultured skin autografts of the neck, genitalia, feet, scalp, face, eyelids, orbits, ears, mouth, hands, and/or multiple digits; autograft of first 25 sq cm or less

15156: additional 1–75 sq cm (list separately in addition to primary procedure code)

15157: each additional 100 square centimeters, each additional 1% of a child's or infant's body area, or any portion thereof (list separately in addition to primary procedure code)

15200: Free full thickness graft, including direct closure of donor site such as the trunk; 20 sq cm or less

15201: each additional 20 sq cm, or portion thereof (list separately in addition to primary procedure code)

15220: Free full thickness graft, including direct closure of donor site, such as the scalp, arms, and/or legs; graft size of 20 sq cm or less

15221: each additional 20 sq cm, or portion thereof (list separately in addition to primary procedure code)

15240: Free full thickness graft, including direct closure of donor site, such as the genitalia, axillae, neck, forehead, cheeks, mouth, chin, hands and/or feet; graft size of 20 sq cm or less

15241: each additional 20 sq cm, or portion thereof (list separately in addition to primary procedure code)

15260: Free full thickness graft, including direct closure of donor site, such as the nose, ears, eyelids, and/or lips; graft size of 20 sq cm or less

15261: each additional 20 sq cm, or portion thereof (list separately in addition to primary procedure code) (Bernard et al., 2015)

Skin Substitute Grafts

15271: Application of skin substitute graft to the trunk, arms, or legs with a total wound surface area of up to 100 sq cm; first 25 sq cm or less wound surface area

15272: each additional 25 sq cm wound surface area, or portion thereof (list separately in addition to the code for the primary procedure)

15273: Application of a skin substitute graft to the trunk, arms, or legs with a total wound surface area larger than or equal to 100

square centimeters; the first 100 square centimeters of the wound surface area, or 1% of an infant's or child's body area

15274: each additional 100 sq cm of the wound surface, or a portion thereof, or each extra 1% of a baby or child's body area, or a portion thereof (list separately in addition to the code for the primary procedure)

15275: Application of skin substitute graft to the scalp, face, eyelids, orbits, ears, mouth, neck, genitalia, feet, hands, and/or multiple digits with a total wound surface area of up to 100 sq cm; first 25 sq cm or less wound surface area

15276: each additional 25 sq cm wound surface area, or portion thereof (list separately in addition to the code for the primary procedure)

15277: Application of skin substitute graft to the scalp, face, ears, eyelids, orbits, neck, hands, genitalia, feet, and/or multiple digits with a total wound surface area greater than or equal to 100 sq cm; first 100 sq cm wound surface area, or 1% of body area of infants or children

15278: each additional 100 sq cm wound surface area, or portion thereof, or each additional 1% of body area of infants and children, or portion thereof (list separately in addition to the code for the primary procedure) (Bernard et al., 2015)

Flaps (Skin and/or Deep Tissues)

The goal of a pedicle flap is to shift tissue to a new location while maintaining blood flow to the relocated tissue. The pedicle flap conceals a defect at the new location. In rare instances, the physician will construct a tubed bridge of tissue between the donor and recipient sites. A blood supply is created at the recipient site over time, and the donor end of the pedicle can be disconnected from its vascular supply. A pedicle flap is also known as an interpolation flap (Bernard et al., 2015).

15570: Formation of direct or tubed pedicle on the trunk, with or without transfer

15572: the scalp, arms, or legs

15574: the forehead, cheeks, chin, mouth, neck, axillae, genitalia, hands, or feet

15576: the eyelids, nose, ears, lips, or intraoral

15600: Delay in developing or sectioning of flap (division and inset) at the trunk

15610: at the scalp, arms, or legs

15620: at the forehead, cheeks, chin, mouth, neck, axillae, genitalia, hands, or feet

15630: at the eyelids, nose, ears, or lips

15650: Intermediate transfer of any pedicle flap on any location (e.g., abdomen to wrist, Walking tube)

15731: Forehead flap with preservation of vascular pedicle (e.g., axial pattern flap, paramedian forehead flap)

15732: Muscle, myocutaneous, or fasciocutaneous flap on the head and neck (e.g., temporalis, masseter muscle, sternocleidomastoid, levator scapulae)

15734:   trunk

15736:   upper extremity

15738:   lower extremity (Bernard et al., 2015)

Other Flaps and Grafts

Microvascular anastomosis is the merging of vessels less than 2 mm in diameter using an operating microscope. A composite graft is made up of multiple types of tissue, such as the cartilaginous skin mix seen in the nostrils and ear. This combination of tissues may be utilized to fill a skin defect and add structural support to the skin. Similarly, derma-fascia-fat grafts are utilized to fill defect pockets and return the flesh to its normal position (Bernard et al., 2015).

15740: Identification and dissection of an anatomically named axial vessel is required for the island pedicle flap

15750:   a neurovascular pedicle

15756: Microvascular anastomosis in a free muscle or myocutaneous flap

15757: Microvascular anastomosis with a free skin flap

15758: Microvascular anastomosis in a free fascial flap

15760: Composite graft (for example, full thickness of external ear or nasal ala) with main donor area closure

15770: derma-fat-fascia

15775: Punch graft for hair transplant; 1–15 punch grafts

15776: greater than 15 punch grafts

15777: The implantation of a biologic implant (such as an acellular dermal matrix) for the strengthening of soft tissue (such as the breast or trunk) (list separately in addition to the code for the primary procedure) (Bernard et al., 2015)

Other Procedures

A chemical peel is a skin exfoliation procedure that involves the application of therapeutically caustic chemicals to the skin. This generates a chemical reaction that results in fewer wrinkles and more uniform skin color, often known as improving cosmesis. Manual dermabrasion produces similar outcomes (Bernard et al., 2015).

15780: Total face dermabrasion (e.g., for acne scarring, fine wrinkling, rhytids, or general keratosis)

15781: segmental, face

15782: regional, other than the face

15783: superficial, any site (e.g., tattoo removal)

15786: Single lesion abrasion (e.g., keratosis, scar)

15787: each additional four lesions or less (list separately in addition to the code for the primary procedure)

15788: Facial, epidermal chemical peel

15789: dermal

15792: Non-facial, epidermal chemical peel

15793: dermal

15819: Cervicoplasty

15820: Lower eyelid blepharoplasty

15821: with extensive herniated fat pad

15822: Upper eyelid blepharoplasty

15823: with excessive skin weighting down lid

15824: Forehead rhytidectomy

15825: and neck with platysmal tightening (platysma flap, P-flap)

15826: and glabellar frown lines

15828: and cheek, chin, and neck

15829: and superficial musculoaponeurotic system (SMAS) flap

15830: Excision of excessive skin and subcutaneous tissue (includes lipectomy) on the abdomen, infraumbilical panniculectomy

15832:   thigh

15833:   leg

15834:   hip

15835:   buttock

15836:   arm

15837:   forearm or hand

15838:   submental fat pad

15839:   other area

15840: Free fascia graft for facial nerve paralysis (including obtaining fascia)

15841:   free muscle graft (including obtaining graft)

15842:   free muscle flap by microsurgical technique

15845:   regional muscle transfer

15847: Excessive skin and subcutaneous tissue removal (including lipectomy), abdominal surgery (e.g., abdominoplasty) (including umbilical transposition and fascial plication) (list separately in addition to the primary procedure code)

15850: Removal of sutures under anesthesia (other than local) with the same surgeon

15851: Removal of sutures under anesthesia (other than local) with another surgeon

15852: Dressing change under anesthesia (other than local) for anything other than burns

15860: Intravenous injection of substance (e.g., fluorescein) to test vascular flow in the flap or graft

15876: Suction assisted lipectomy of the head or neck

15877:   trunk

15878:   upper extremity

15879:   lower extremity (Bernard et al., 2015)

Pressure Ulcers (Decubitus Ulcers)

Decubitus ulcers are localized wounds brought on by persistent pressure on the skin. A common decubitus ulcer is seen in a bedridden, wheelchair-bound, or otherwise immobile patient. When blood circulation is impaired due to persistent pressure, the skin begins to deteriorate, and an ulcer may form. The ulcer usually forms over a bony protrusion. If a more conservative treatment does not work, the ulcer may be excised. To assist wound closure, surgical excision of the ulcer may be combined with the creation of a skin flap. In some circumstances, bone is extracted (Bernard et al., 2015).

15920: Excision of a coccygeal pressure ulcer with coccygectomy with primary suture

15922: with flap closure

15931: Excision of a sacral pressure ulcer with primary suture

15933: with ostectomy

15934: Excision of a sacral pressure ulcer with skin flap closure

15935: with ostectomy

15936: Sacral pressure ulcer excision in preparation for closure of a muscle or myocutaneous flap or a skin graft

15937: with ostectomy

15940: Excisions of ischial pressure ulcer with primary suture

15941: with ostectomy (ischiectomy)

15944: Excision of ischial pressure ulcer with skin flap closure

What code is used to report the implantation of a biologic implant (such as an acellular dermal matrix) for the strengthening of soft tissue?

15945:   with ostectomy

15946: Ischial pressure ulcer excision with ostectomy to prepare for muscle or myocutaneous flap or skin graft closure

15950: Excision of trochanteric pressure ulcer with primary suture

15951:   with ostectomy

15952: Excision of trochanteric pressure ulcer with skin flap closure

15953:   with ostectomy

15956: Trochanteric pressure ulcer excision in preparation for closure of a muscle or myocutaneous flap or a skin graft

15958:   with ostectomy (Bernard et al., 2015)

Burns, Local Treatment

Burns occur when the skin is injured by a heat source. Electrical current, chemicals, fire, hot liquid, and radiation are all common sources of burn-causing heat. The burn may just harm the outermost skin and subcutaneous tissue, or it may reach the bronchial tubes, lungs, or other organs. This series of codes is intended to report only the local treatment of the burned surface (Bernard et al., 2015).

16000: Initial treatment for a first-degree burn when nothing more than local treatment is needed

16020: Dressings and/or debridement of initial or subsequent partial-thickness burns; size small (less than 5% of total body surface area)

16025: medium size burns (e.g., whole face or whole extremity, or 5–10% of total body surface area)

16030: large size burns (e.g., more than one extremity, or greater than 10% of total body surface area)

16035: Initial incision escharotomy

16036: each additional incision should be listed separately in addition to the primary procedure code (Bernard et al., 2015)

Destruction: 17000–17380

Destruction, Benign or Premalignant Lesions

Electrodesiccation, electrofulguration, liquid nitrogen freeze, laser, or chemical treatment can all be used to successfully eliminate some skin lesions. This section includes codes for reporting benign or premalignant lesions like condylomata, papillomata, molluscum contagiosum, herpetic lesions, plantar and flat warts, milia, and actinic keratoses. These destructions may take place simultaneously with curetting. Other chapters of the CPT code set have assigned site-specific skin destruction codes to the mouth, genitalia, anus, eyelid, and conjunctiva. These codes would be reported instead of 17000–17250, as applicable. There are also codes for corns and calluses (11055–11057) (Bernard et al., 2015).

17000: First lesion destruction (e.g., laser surgery, electrosurgery, cryosurgery, chemosurgery, surgical curettement) of premalignant lesions

17003:   2–14 lesions, each (list separately in addition to code for the first lesion)

17004: 15 or more lesions destruction (e.g., laser surgery, electrosurgery, cryosurgery, chemosurgery, surgical curettement) of premalignant lesions

17106: Cutaneous vascular proliferative lesion destruction (e.g., laser technique); less than 1o sq cm

17107:   10.0–50.0 sq cm

17108:   over 50.0 sq cm

17110: Destruction of up to 14 benign lesions other than skin tags or cutaneous vascular proliferative lesions

17111:   15 or more lesions

17250: Chemical cauterization of granulation tissue (pound flesh, sinus, or fistula) (Bernard et al., 2015)

Destruction, Malignant Lesions, Any Method

Any combination of cryosurgery, laser, electrosurgery, or chemical treatment can be used in conjunction with curettage to surgically remove a malignant lesion. The code is assigned depending on the anatomical location and size of the malignant lesion, such as basal or squamous cell carcinoma. Topical fluorouracil application is not recorded as destruction but it may be included in services offered with an E/M service (Bernard et al., 2015).

17260: Destruction of malignant lesions (e.g., laser surgery, electrosurgery, cryosurgery, chemosurgery, surgical curettement) on the trunk, arms, or legs with a lesion diameter of 0.5 cm or less

17261: lesion diameter 0.6–1.0 cm

17262: lesion diameter 1.1–2.0 cm

17263: lesion diameter 2.1–3.0 cm

17264: lesion diameter 3.1–4.0 cm

17266: lesion diameter greater than 4.0 cm

17270: Destruction of malignant lesions (e.g., laser surgery, electrosurgery, cryosurgery, chemosurgery, or surgical curettement) on the scalp, neck, hands, feet, genitalia, with a lesion diameter of 0.5 cm or less

17271: lesion diameter 0.6–1.0 cm

17272: lesion diameter 1.1–2.0 cm

17273: lesion diameter 2.1–3.0 cm

17274: lesion diameter 3.1–4.0 cm

17276: lesion diameter greater than 4.0 cm

17280: Destruction of malignant lesions (e.g., laser surgery, electro-surgery, cryosurgery, chemosurgery, or surgical curettement) on the face, ears, eyelids, nose, lips, mucous membrane with a lesion diameter of 0.5 cm or less

17281: lesion diameter 0.6–1.0 cm

17282: lesion diameter 1.1–2.0 cm

17283: lesion diameter 2.1–3.0 cm

17284: lesion diameter 3.1–4.0 cm

17286: lesion diameter greater than 4.0 cm (Bernard et al., 2015)

Mohs Microbiology Surgery

Mohs micrographic surgery (MMS) is a surgical method in which many excisions and microscopic exams are performed to verify that the entire lesion is eliminated with the optimal cosmetic and therapeutic benefit. During the surgery, the surgeon acts as a pathologist, inspecting each layer removed. Layers are excised one at a time until the whole lesion along with a healthy tissue margin is destroyed. An MMS "block" is a slice of tissue that has been produced, embedded in a mounting medium, and microscopically analyzed (Bernard et al., 2015).

17311: Mohs micrographic technique, which includes the removal of all gross tumors, surgical excision of tissue specimens, mapping, color coding of specimens, microscopic examination of specimens by the surgeon, and histopathologic preparation including routine stain(s) (e.g., hematoxylin and eosin, toluidine blue). This technique involves the head, neck, hands, feet, genitalia, or any location with surgery directly involving muscle, cartilage, bone, tendon, major nerves, or vessels; the first stage of up to five tissue blocks

17312: each additional stage after the first stage, up to five tissue blocks (list separately in addition to the code for the primary procedure)

17313: Mohs micrographic technique, which includes the removal of all gross tumors, surgical excision of tissue specimens, mapping, color coding of specimens, microscopic examination of specimens by the surgeon, and histopathologic preparation including routine stain(s) (e.g., hematoxylin and eosin, toluidine blue). This code is specifically for the trunk, arms, or legs; the first stage of up to five tissue blocks

17314: each additional stage after the first stage, up to five tissue blocks (list separately in addition to the code for primary procedure)

17315: Mohs micrographic technique, which includes the removal of all gross tumors, surgical excision of tissue specimens, mapping, color coding of specimens, microscopic examination of specimens by the surgeon, and histopathologic preparation including routine stain(s) (e.g., hematoxylin and eosin, toluidine blue). This code is used for each additional block after the first five tissue blocks at any stage (list separately in addition to the code for the primary procedure) (Bernard et al., 2015)

Other Procedures

17340: Cryotherapy (CO2 slush, liquid N2) for acne

17360: Chemical exfoliation for acne (e.g., acne paste, acid)

17380: Electrolysis epilation, each 30 minutes (Bernard et al., 2015)

Breast: 19000–19396

Incision

A breast cyst puncture aspiration is a diagnostic technique that may also have therapeutic benefits for the patient because it decompresses what could be a painful cyst (Bernard et al., 2015).

19000: Puncture aspiration of breast cyst

19001: each additional cyst should be listed separately in addition to the code for the primary procedure

19020: Mastotomy with exploration or drainage of deep abscess

19030: Injection procedure only used for mammary ductogram, or galactogram (Bernard et al., 2015)

Excision

During a breast biopsy, all or a portion of a lesion is removed without regard for surgical margin adequacy. There is documentation of surgical margin care in breast excision. Even when there is no breast involvement, chest wall tumor codes 19260–19272 are reported with codes from the Breast section (Bernard et al., 2015).

19081: Percutaneous breast biopsy with the insertion of breast localization device(s) (e.g., clip, metallic pellet), and imaging of the biopsy specimen when performed, first lesion including stereotactic guidance

19082: each additional lesion, with stereotactic guidance (list separately in addition to primary procedure code)

19083: Percutaneous breast biopsy with placement of breast localization device(s) (e.g., clip, metallic pellet) and imaging of the biopsy specimen when performed, first lesion including ultrasound guidance

19084: each additional lesion, with ultrasound guidance (list separately in addition to primary procedure code)

19085: Percutaneous breast biopsy with breast localization device(s) placement (e.g., clip, metallic pellet) and biopsy specimen imaging when biopsy is performed, primary lesion with magnetic resonance guidance

19086: each additional lesion, with magnetic resonance guidance (list separately in addition to primary procedure code)

19100: Percutaneous breast biopsy using needle core, without imaging guidance (separate procedure)

19101: open, incisional

19105: Ablation, cryosurgical, of each fibroadenoma, including ultrasound guidance

19110: Exploration of the nipple with or without excision of a single lactiferous duct or a papilloma lactiferous duct

19112: Excision of lactiferous duct fistula

19120: Cyst, fibroadenoma; or other benign or malignant tumor, abnormal breast tissue, duct lesion, nipple, or areola lesion excision (except 19300), open on male or female with one or more lesions

19125: Excision of breast lesion identified by preoperative placement of radiological marker, open; single lesion

19126: each additional lesion discovered by a preoperative radiological marker should be recorded separately from the primary procedure code

19260: Chest wall tumor excision including ribs

19271: Chest wall tumor excision involving ribs with plastic reconstruction; without mediastinal lymphadenectomy

19272: with mediastinal lymphadenectomy (Bernard et al., 2015)

Introduction

A wire, clip, or pellet may be put into the lesion prior to a breast biopsy to help identify the lesion during the excision procedure. This insertion may need radiological guidance. The type of guidance and the number of lesions localized influence code selection (Bernard et al., 2015).

19281: Percutaneous placement of breast localization device(s) (e.g., clip, metallic pellet, wire/needle, or radioactive seeds), first lesion including mammographic guidance

19282: each additional lesion including mammographic guidance (list separately in addition to the code for the primary procedure)

19283: Percutaneous insertion of breast localization device(s) (e.g., clip, metallic pellet, wire/needle, or radioactive seeds), first lesion including stereotactic guidance

19284: for each additional lesion using stereotactic guidance (list separately in addition to the code for the primary procedure)

19285: Percutaneous insertion of breast localization device(s) (e.g., clip, metallic pellet, wire/needle, or radioactive seeds), first lesion including ultrasound guidance

19286: each additional lesion using ultrasound guidance (list separately in addition to the code for the primary procedure)

19287: Percutaneous insertion of breast localization device(s) (e.g., clip, metallic pellet, wire/needle, or radioactive seeds), first lesion using magnetic resonance guidance

19288: each additional lesion using magnetic resonance guidance (list separately in addition to the code for the primary procedure)

19296: Application of interstitial radioelements after partial mastectomy using a radiotherapy afterloading expandable catheter (single or multichannel) on a date distinct from the partial mastectomy; incorporates imaging guidance

19297: concurrent with partial mastectomy (list separately in addition to the code for the primary procedure)

19298: Using imaging guidance, radiation afterloading brachytherapy catheters (of the multiple tube and button type) are inserted into the breast for the application of interstitial radioelements after (at the time of or after) partial mastectomy (Bernard et al., 2015)

Mastectomy Procedures

A substantial quantity of breast tissue and some skin are removed during a partial mastectomy. The entire breast is removed in a simple, complete mastectomy, but the lymph nodes and surrounding muscles are spared. Subcutaneous mastectomy is a surgical procedure that removes the tumor and breast tissue while leaving the nipple and skin of the breast intact. The radical mastectomy codes are chosen based on which lymph nodes and muscles are excised along with the breast. Based on the excision stated in the operative report, a total mastectomy should be documented using a code from the range 19303–19307 (Bernard et al., 2015).

19300: Mastectomy for gynecomastia

19301: Partial mastectomy (e.g., lumpectomy, tylectomy, quadrantectomy, segmentectomy);

19302: with axillary lymphadenectomy

19303: Simple, complete mastectomy

19304: Subcutaneous mastectomy

19305: Radical mastectomy including pectoral muscles and axillary lymph nodes

19306: Radical mastectomy including pectoral muscles, axillary and internal mammary lymph nodes (Urban type operation)

19307: Modified radical mastectomy involving axillary lymph nodes, with or without pectoralis minor muscle, but without the pectoralis major muscle (Bernard et al., 2015)

Repair and/or Reconstruction

Breast shapes can be modified surgically for cosmetic or therapeutic purposes. The nipple is moved to a higher position on the breast during a mastopexy, which involves surgically lifting a breast that has ptosis. Fat, tissue, and skin may be removed or altered during mammaplasty to reduce the size of the breasts or to improve the appearance of the breast. Implants are used in some mammaplasties to augment breast size (Bernard et al., 2015).

19316: Mastopexy

19318: Mammaplasty for reduction

19324: Mammaplasty, or breast augmentation without the use of a prosthetic implant

19325: with prosthetic implant

19328: Removing the intact mammary implant

19330: Mammary implant material removal

19340: Breast prosthesis insertion immediately after mastopexy, mastectomy, or reconstruction

19342: Breast prosthesis insertion is delayed after mastopexy, mastectomy, or reconstruction

19350: Reconstruction of the nipple/areola

19355: Inverted nipple correction

19357: Breast reconstruction with tissue expander, either immediate or delayed, including later expansion

19361: Breast reconstruction with a latissimus dorsi flap but without the use of a prosthetic implant

19364: Breast reconstruction using a free flap

19366: Breast reconstruction using a different technique

19367: Transverse rectus abdominis myocutaneous flap (TRAM) breast reconstruction on a single pedicle, including donor site closure

19368: with microvascular anastomosis (supercharging)

19369: Breast reconstruction using a transverse rectus abdominis myocutaneous flap (TRAM) on a double pedicle, as well as donor site closure

19370: Breast surgery using an open periprosthetic capsulotomy

19371: Periprosthetic capsulotomy on the breast

19380: Review of a breast that has undergone reconstruction

19396: Preparation of moulage for customized breast implant

2.2 Musculoskeletal System: 20100–29999

Muscle, bone, and other connective tissue make up the musculo-skeletal system. There are over 200 bones in an adult's body which, when articulated, provide structure and mobility. Bones also protect organs; for example, the skull protects the brain just like the sternum protects the heart. Calcium and phosphorus, which are necessary minerals for cellular activity throughout the body, are stored in bones. Physical stress or damage (such as exercise or simply the weight of our bodies) and hormones and other substances flowing in the blood throughout life cause bone remodeling. Bone remodeling modifies bone architecture to meet changing mechanical needs and aids in the repair of microdamages in the bone matrix, preventing the accumulation of old bone. It is also vital in maintaining plasma calcium homeostasis (Bernard et al., 2015).

Blood vessels and nerves are accommodated by bones along depressions or openings. These anatomical areas are also given names based on their function. A fissure, for example, is a thin passageway; a fontanel, a space between skull bones; a foramen, a round opening; a fossa, a shallow depression; a fovea, a small, deep depression; a sinus, a bony tube; and a sulcus is a long, narrow groove. Tendons are connective tissues that run from muscle to bone. Cartilage is a soft tissue that spreads from the surface of a bone at a joint to reduce friction during movement (Bernard et al., 2015).

There are different degrees of joint flexion. Synovial joints have a lot of mobility, cartilaginous joints have little movement, and fibrous joints are immovable. The fibrous joints in the skull, for example, are flexible at birth but immobile in adulthood. Costal cartilage connects the ribs 8–10 to the sternum. The connection between the rib and the sternum has limited flexibility, allowing the rib cage to expand during respiration. Cartilaginous joints connect the vertebrae as well. The most prevalent joints in the body are synovial joints. These joints are surrounded by tough ligaments that provide strength and support and are sealed in a synovial membrane that produces lubricating fluid. A bursa is a fluid-filled sac that reduces friction between two synovial joint components (Bernard et al., 2015).

Fascia encloses each muscle or muscle grouping, allowing it to move independently of surrounding tissue. Skeletal muscle contracts in response to electrical impulses from spinal cord motor neurons.

When a muscle contracts, the tendons to which it is attached pull on the bone, generating bone movement. The name of a muscle may be derived from its attachments, such as the sternocleidomastoid muscle, which connects the sternum and clavicle to the mastoid bone. Others are named from their location, such as the orbicularis oculi muscle, which is positioned at the orbit (Bernard et al., 2015).

All arthroscopic procedures are separated in the Musculoskeletal System code set, which appears near the end of the section. Codes used to report procedures conducted on bone marrow are excluded from the Musculoskeletal System code set. These procedures are coded using the Hemic and Lymphatic Systems coding set (Bernard et al., 2015).

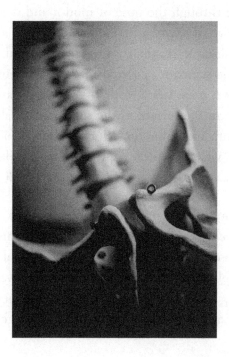

2.3 Respiratory System: 30000-32999

In the most basic terms, oxygen is necessary at the cellular level in order to make energy from the food that we ingest; this is equivalent to a fire needing oxygen to burn. The respiratory system carries oxygen from the surrounding environment to the circulation, where it is then delivered to individual cells throughout the body. Carbon dioxide, an important byproduct of energy production, is also transported back to the respiratory system via the bloodstream. Each inspiration (breath in) brings oxygen-rich air into the body, and each expiration (breath out) expels carbon dioxide and other gaseous waste products (Bernard et al., 2015).

Air is pulled in through the nose or mouth and is moisturized and warmed in the nasal cavity as it moves. The nose is surrounded by four pairs of sinuses: maxillary, frontal, sphenoid, and ethmoid. Sinuses are bone structures covered in mucous membranes. Mucus is produced by the sinuses and drains into the nasal structure via the ostia. Cilia on the surface of the sinus and nasal epithelium filter particles from incoming air. Mucus produced in the nose and sinuses collects what has been deposited on the cilia, and the cilia delivers the mucus to the pharynx (Bernard et al., 2015).

The lungs expand greatly upon inspiration. Pleural membranes line the lungs, reducing thoracic friction during inspiration and expiration. These membranes are called the inner visceral pleura and the outer parietal pleura. Lubricating fluid exists between these membranes, allowing the lungs to move freely throughout the thorax. The lungs are not exact replicas of one another. The right lung contains three lobes, while the left lung only has two since it shares space with the heart (Bernard et al., 2015).

A considerable proportion of respiratory disorders are surgically addressed. The nose is frequently the point of impact in an injury due to its prominence on the face. The nasal septum, as well as the paired nasal bones and local cartilage, are all easily damaged. Sinus hyperplasia, which impairs function, can be caused by inflammation. The lungs must be a closed system in order to work properly, and if air can escape, they will fail to expand, much like a balloon being blown up. This is known as pneumothorax, and it can be treated surgically (Bernard et al., 2015).

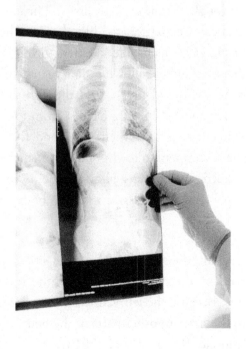

2.4 Cardiovascular System: 33016–37799

The body's main transportation route system is the cardiovascular system. Its main function is to move carbon dioxide from the cells back to the lungs and to carry oxygen from the lungs to the cells. Other items carried by the cardiovascular system include nutrients, antibodies, and waste materials. The capillaries, veins, venules, arteries, and heart make up the cardiovascular system. The heart is responsible for the circulation of blood throughout the body. The heart has four chambers: the right and left atria, as well as the right and left ventricles. The right and left halves of a healthy heart do not interact directly (Bernard et al., 2015).

Blood moves through the heart as follows. Through the superior and inferior vena cava, deoxygenated blood enters the right atrium. When the tricuspid valve opens, blood enters the right ventricle. The pulmonary valve then opens, allowing deoxygenated blood to enter the pulmonary artery. Blood then passes through the lungs, depositing carbon dioxide and absorbing oxygen from the capillary beds. The pulmonary vein returns oxygenated blood to the left atrium. The mitral valve then opens, allowing blood to enter the left ventricle. Finally, the aortic valve opens, allowing the powerful ventricular muscle to pump blood up and out into the body (Bernard et al., 2015).

Aside from the pulmonary arteries, arteries transport oxygenated blood. Veins transmit deoxygenated blood, with the exception of the pulmonary veins. Because the left ventricle is in charge of transporting blood from the heart to other parts of the body, it has the largest and strongest muscles (Bernard et al., 2015).

2.5 Hemic and Lymphatic Systems: 38100–38999

Procedures involving the spleen, bone marrow and stem cells, and lymph nodes are all part of the hemic and lymphatic system. The spleen is structurally similar to the lymph nodes and functions as a blood filter (hence the term 'hemic'). Codes for splenectomies, spleen repair, and spleen diagnostic laparoscopies can be found here. Procedures for extracting, storing, and preparing bone marrow for transplant are covered by bone marrow codes (as in the case of leukemia patients). The term "hematopoietic," which refers to stem cells that produce blood cells, can be used to identify stem cells found in bone marrow (Medical Billing and Coding, 2022).

The lymphatic system is made up of nodes located throughout the body. If you've ever had a sore throat, you've undoubtedly experienced swollen lymph nodes. Lymph nodes, like the spleen, function as blood filters and store B and T cells, the immune system's frontline fighters. Despite the importance of the lymphatic system in the immune system, there are only a few procedures listed under its subsection. Excision, drainage (incision), laparoscopy, and radical resection (the complete removal of the lymph nodes) are all coded (Medical Billing and Coding, 2022).

38100-38200 Surgical Procedures on the Spleen

Excision: 38100-38102

The normal spleen is around the size of a fist and is extensively vascularized. A splenectomy can be either total or partial. An open splenectomy (codes 38100–38102) is typically performed in an emergency or when direct visualization and exploration is required, such as after a traumatic injury (Bernard et al., 2015).

Repair: 38115

The spleen is shielded by a strong outer capsule. This capsule bursts, allowing the highly vascularized tissue inside to bleed into the abdomen. A ruptured spleen is frequently caused by blunt trauma and can be treated using suture repair (splenorrhaphy), or a total or partial splenectomy (Bernard et al., 2015).

Laparoscopy: 38120

38120: Laparoscopy, surgical, splenectomy (Bernard et al., 2015)

Introduction: 38200

Splenoportography is the introduction of radiopaque material into the spleen to improve radiographic visualization of the splenic and main portal veins of the portal circulation (Bernard et al., 2015).

38204–38232 General Surgical Procedures on the Hemic and Lymphatic Systems

Bone Marrow or Stem Cell Services/Procedures

Bone marrow transplants are used to treat leukemia, lymphoma, breast cancer, multiple myeloma, renal cell carcinoma, neuroblastoma, ovarian cancer, aplastic anemia, inherited inborn metabolic disorders, and immunodeficiencies. The harvesting and modification processes differ based on the type of cell required (Bernard et al., 2015).

38240–38243 Transplantation and Post-Transplantation Cellular Infusions

HPCs (hematopoietic progenitor cells) are also known as stem cells. The code for each allogeneic stem cell transplant, whether they come from cord blood, blood-derived peripheral stem cells, or bone marrow, is coded 38240. Code 38241 is used to report the infusion of cells obtained from the same patient at an earlier time. Code 38243 is used to describe an HPC boost given as a result of complications after the administration of marrow suppressive drugs to restore normal blood counts in post-transplant patients with infection. Donor lymphocyte infusions (DLIs) to treat relapse or viral infections in allogeneic transplant recipients are reported using code 38242 (Bernard et al., 2015).

38300-38999 Surgical Procedures on Lymph Nodes and Lymphatic Channels

Incision: 38300-38382

The thoracic duct, also known as the left lymphatic duct, alimentary duct, chyliferous duct, or Van Hoorne's canal, is the biggest lymphatic channel. The thoracic duct runs from the abdomen to the neck, paralleling the spinal column. The action of breathing causes lymph within the duct to push forward (Bernard et al., 2015).

Excision: 38500-38555

The sentinel node is the first lymph node to drain away from the site of a tumor. Metastatic cancer typically begins in the sentinel node before spreading to other regions of the body. The sentinel node is frequently examined during the staging of a tumor. Open biopsy of a sentinel node normally involves two codes: code 38792 for the injection procedure that identifies the sentinel node, and a code from the code range 38500–38542 for the excision (Bernard et al., 2015).

Limited Lymphadenectomy for Staging: 38562-38564

The evaluation of a tumor to evaluate the severity and degree of metastasis is referred to as staging. Cancer cells can escape from the primary tumor and reach the bloodstream or lymphatic system. Sampling of regional lymph nodes for metastatic disease may be part of staging to inform the primary cancer treatment plan (Bernard et al., 2015).

Laparoscopy: 38570–38589

Laparoscopy is a surgical technique that includes entering the body through several small portals and performing surgery with tools, optics, and lights inserted through these portals. It is less invasive than open surgical procedures; however, it does not allow for direct visualization. Sampling of regional lymph nodes for metastatic disease may be part of staging to inform the primary cancer treatment plan (Bernard et al., 2015).

Radical Lymphadenectomy (Radical Resection of Lymph Nodes): 38700–38780

The lymphatic system is one of the primary pathways via which cancer can spread. The head and neck contain nearly one-third of all lymph nodes. A radical (full) neck dissection (RND) or a modified radical neck dissection (MRND) may be suggested in the treatment of head and neck cancer. Because the purpose of the neck dissection is to limit disease progression, various non-lymphatic structures (e.g., muscles, glands, arteries, and/or veins) may be removed depending on how far the cancer has traveled. Suprahyoid lymphadenectomy and supraomohyoid lymphadenectomy are procedures that are sometimes documented as suprahyoid/supraomohyoid neck dissection. Lymphadenectomy is a unilateral operation. Because there is no single code for resection of a primary tumor with a modified radical neck dissection, one code (e.g., 42420) is used to report the tumor resection and another code is used to record the modified radical neck dissection (e.g.,code 38724) (Bernard et al., 2015).

Introduction: 38790–38794

An open biopsy of a sentinel node is coded with two codes: 38792 for the injection procedure that identifies the sentinel node and a code from the range 38500–38542 for the excision (Bernard et al., 2015).

Other Procedures: 38900

When conducted, intraoperative identification (e.g., mapping) of sentinel lymph node(s) includes injection of a non-radioactive dye. (List separately in addition to primary procedure code) (Bernard et al., 2015).

2.6 Digestive System: 40490–49999

The digestive system is in charge of food intake, digestion, and assimilation, as well as the disposal of residual digestive waste products. Food enters the mouth and passes through the alimentary tract in a continuous pathway from mouth to esophagus to the stomach to small intestine into the large intestine to the rectum and finally to anus. Nutrients have been transported into the circulatory system by the time food reaches the large intestine, leaving only waste in the form of feces behind. Furthermore, the large intestine is vital in water balance because it absorbs a substantial amount of water and electrolytes (particularly sodium). These bacteria release a lot of gas while breaking down things in the large intestine. Other digestive organs (liver, pancreas, and gallbladder) connect with the alimentary tract via ducts to provide digestion enzymes and bile (Bernard et al., 2015).

The stomach regulates how quickly food reaches the small intestines. It also serves as a temporary storage space for food and is the first section of the gastrointestinal tract to break down proteins into peptides. Food subsequently flows via the pyloric valve into the small intestine's duodenum. The small intestine is divided into three sections: the duodenum, jejunum, and ileum. Pancreatic enzymes and bile, which originate in the liver and are stored and released by the gallbladder, also contribute to the digestion of food in the duodenum. When food reaches the jejunum and ileum, it is further broken down for absorption into the bloodstream. What is left is waste and water (Bernard et al., 2015).

The small intestine empties into the large intestine via the ileocecal valve, which empties into the ascending colon's cecum. Water is taken from waste as it passes through the ascending colon, transverse colon, and descending colon, which is connected to the rectum. Nerves in the rectum signal the brain to the urge to defecate. This urge is controlled by the anal sphincter (Bernard et al., 2015).

When a person eats, the gallbladder contracts, allowing bile to be released into ducts that flow into the common bile duct. The ampulla of Vater sphincter relaxes, allowing bile to pass into the duodenum. Bile flows directly from the liver after the gallbladder is removed, with no functional change. In addition to digesting enzymes, the pancreas is an endocrine gland that generates insulin, glucagon, somatostatin, and pancreatic polypeptides. Endoscopy is a common surgical method for both diagnostic and therapeutic treatments since the gastrointestinal system is essentially a continuous lumen with a few connecting ducts (Bernard et al., 2015).

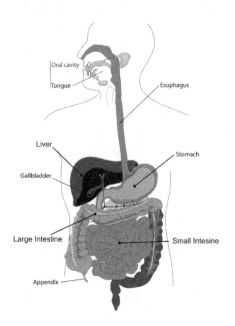

2.7 Urinary System: 50010–53899

The kidneys, ureters, urinary bladder, and urethra comprise the urinary system. The kidneys filter metabolic wastes, excess ions, and chemicals from the blood to produce urine, which is excreted from the body via micturition (urination). The urinary system is made up of the ureters, the urinary bladder, and the urethra, which drain urine from the kidneys, store it, and then release it during urination. The urinary system not only filters and eliminates wastes from the body but also maintains the homeostasis of water, ions (potassium, sodium, calcium, magnesium, phosphate, and chloride ions), pH, blood pressure, and calcium. The glomeruli of the paired kidneys, each connected to a ureter that transports waste (urine) to the bladder, filter the urine (Bernard et al., 2015).

Once the waste fluid has been filtered by the kidney nephrons, it converges at the renal pelvis, which narrows to join the ureter, a foot-long channel that empties urine into the bladder. The bladder is a hollow, muscular organ that can hold up to 400 milliliters of urine when stretched. When the bladder's muscle walls reach capacity, they tell the brain that it is time to micturate. Urine is released into the hollow urethra and released from the body to empty the bladder. The internal urinary sphincter (IUS) and the external urinary sphincter (EUS) govern urine release. The internal urethral sphincter is located near the bottom of the bladder and prevents urine from leaking into the urethra (Bernard et al., 2015).

Urinary blockage is a typical condition in the renal system. Obstruction in the urinary route can occur anywhere: in the kidney, ureter, bladder, or urethra. The obstruction could be caused by a tumor, stenosis, or congenital deformity, or it could be caused by a kidney or ureteral calculus. The stones, also known as nephrolithiasis or ureterolithiasis, are most likely caused by two factors: excessive levels of calcium, oxalate, and uric acid in the bloodstream, which cause crystal formation, or calcium plaque that accumulates in the subepithelial space of the renal papilla. The obstruction caused by a stone is removed if the stone passed naturally. When a stone does not pass on its own, surgery may be required, especially if the obstruction is considerable or if an infection is present. A cystoscope or a percutaneous, laparoscopic, or open technique can be used to remove a stone (Bernard et al., 2015).

2.8 Reproductive System Procedures: 55920

The 54000–58999 section contains procedure codes for the male genital system, reproductive system and intersex, and female genital system. Because of the system's simplicity, the male genital system has the smallest set of codes. The prostate, testes, seminal vesicles, vas deferens, and penis comprise the male genital system. Look for the prefix "orchi-" in procedures performed on the testes. Codes for penile repairs, particularly those involving the urinary opening, can be found in the male genital system section of Surgery. There are also codes for procedures performed on the prostate, such as biopsies and excisions. The section on the male genital system is brief and straightforward. You only need to understand the fundamentals of anatomy (Medical Billing and Coding, 2022).

Procedure codes for the placement of needles or catheters into the pelvis can be found in a very brief set of general "reproductive system" codes. These codes do not discriminate between male and female patients. The female genital system is far more complex than the male genital system. The uterus, ovaries, fallopian tubes, cervix, and vagina comprise the female genital system. When looking for vaginal procedures, look for the prefix "colpo-," whereas uterine procedures use the prefix "hystero-," as in hysterectomy (Medical Billing and Coding, 2022).

2.9 Endocrine System: 60000–60699

The endocrine system constantly analyzes the hormone levels in your blood. Hormones send messages by bonding to the cells they target and relaying the message. When hormone levels rise, the pituitary gland signals other glands to stop producing and releasing hormones. When hormone levels fall below a specific threshold, the pituitary gland can direct other glands to produce and release additional hormones (Cleveland Clinic, 2020).

Hormones influence practically every bodily activity, including:

- Development and growth

- Mood and emotions

- Sexual function and fertility

- Sleep

- Blood pressure

Sometimes glands produce too much or too few hormones. Weight gain, high blood pressure, and changes in sleep, mood, and behavior can all result from this imbalance. Many factors can influence how your body produces and releases hormones. A hormone imbalance can be caused by illness, stress, or certain medications (Cleveland Clinic, 2020).

2.10 Nervous System: 61000-64999

The nervous system is divided into two parts: one is the central nervous system (CNS), which is the body's control center, and the other is the peripheral nervous system (PNS), which consists of cranial and spinal nerves and ganglia, which senses physiologic and environmental stimuli, sends the information to the CNS, and reacts to CNS directives. The CNS is made up of membranes called meninges that surround the spinal cord, cerebrum, cerebellum, diencephalon, and brain stem. Cerebrospinal fluid (CSF) fills the meninges. For protection, the brain and spinal cord are enclosed within the skull and bone vertebrae. The CSF acts as a protective cushion and circulates in the brain and spinal cord to deliver nutrition and remove waste (Bernard et al., 2015).

The cerebrum contains two hemispheres and regulates higher-level thinking. Each hemisphere controls the contralateral body; for example, damage to the right side of the brain may result in weakness in the left side of the body. Each hemisphere is divided into four lobes and controls specific bodily functions: frontal—motor control, learning, planning, and some speech; parietal—somatic and voluntary sensory function; occipital—vision; and temporal—hearing and some speech (Bernard et al., 2015).

The vertebral canal contains the spinal cord. The immediately adjacent and superior vertebrae identify a position on the spinal cord. The spinal cord serves as a link between the CNS and the PNS. Nerve roots are the nerves that connect the PNS to the spinal cord or brain. From the brainstem and the highest level of the spinal cord twelve pairs of nerve roots emerge. The remainder of the spinal cord is made up of 31 pairs of nerve roots. There are two types of PNS systems: afferent and efferent. Afferent nerves transport messages from the PNS to the brain, whereas efferent nerves carry messages from the brain to muscles and other tissue (Bernard et al., 2015).

Any interruption in the neural pathway may result in sensory and/or motor impairment. These disruptions can be minor, such as a compressed medial nerve in the wrist that causes tingling in the fingers, or major, such as a vertebral fracture that causes an injury to the spinal column at the second cervical vertebra and causes incontinence and an inability to move or feel sensations in the trunk, arms, or legs (Bernard et al., 2015).

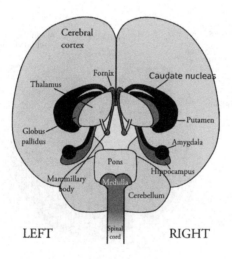

2.11 Eye and Ear: 65091–69979

The eyeball is a complicated organ that rests in the eye socket, also known as the orbit. The orbit is a deep, bony depression in the skull that protects the eyeball. The orbit contains the optic nerve, extraocular muscles, and ocular vasculature, in addition to the fat pads that cushion the eye. The orbit, along with the lids, extraocular muscles, lacrimal system, and conjunctiva, is referred to as an ocular adnexa, or an auxiliary structure to the globe. While some CPT codes in the

Eye and Ocular Adnexa section are used to indicate orbital therapeutic treatment, other orbital codes are found in the Musculoskeletal System code set. Procedures conducted purely on the skin of the eye may also be recorded using Integumentary System codes, and some eye-related surgeries may also be reported using Respiratory System and Nervous System codes (Bernard et al., 2015).

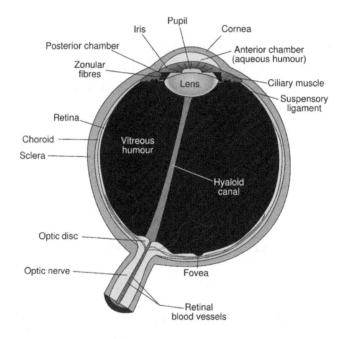

The visual pathway has been known to be an important component of current eye surgery. Lasers changed eye care when it was discovered that a concentrated beam of light emitted by a laser could be used to treat a wide range of ocular abnormalities. A thermal laser beam can be directed at a target in the eye from its position outside the eye. The laser passes through the cornea, lens, aqueous humor, and vitreous humor without causing any damage to them. When the beam reaches the target tissue, it may close blood arteries, eliminate tumors, reattach retinas, or open new pathways for aqueous humor flow. The photodisruption laser is another form of laser that is used to 'treat problems in the clear tissue of the cornea, vitreous humor, or lens (Bernard et al., 2015).

If the surgeon has a clear visual pathway to the deformity, laser surgery is frequently chosen because it avoids many of the dangers involved with open eye surgery. When laser surgery is not an option, the most frequent methods of entering the eye are via a limbal incision or a pars plana approach. A limbal incision is a tiny cut made by the surgeon into the junction of the cornea and the sclera (limbus). If necessary, this minor cut can be sutured after surgery. To remove the lens and/or replace it with an intraocular lens (IOL), a limbal incision is usually performed. The posterior segment is entered via a site posterior to the limbus and the ciliary body in a pars plana approach (Bernard et al., 2015).

Many ocular operations do not necessitate globe penetration. These procedures may be performed to treat strabismus (improper eye alignment), which is frequent in youngsters, or to treat eyelid disorders like ectropion, entropion, or ptosis, which is common in the older population (Bernard et al., 2015).

Formative Assessment Questions:

1. What are the three types of coding guidelines?

2. How much percent would you need to score on the practice test to be prepared to pass the CPC exam?

3. Describe the process of the formation of the nail

4. Why is open biopsy of a sentinel node coded with two codes?

5. How does the production of too much or too few hormones affect the body?

Key Concepts

Integumentary System
- Skin, nails, hair, sebaceous and sudoriferous glands, and the breasts all belong to the integumentary system.

- **Skin, Subcutaneous, and Accessory Structures:** 10030 – 11646

- **Nails:** 11719 – 11765

- **Pilonidal Cyst:** 11770–11772

- **Introduction:** 11900–11983

- **Repair (Closure):** 12001–16036

- **Destruction:** 17000–17380

- **Breast:** 19000–19396

Musculoskeletal System
- Muscle, bone, and other connective tissue make up the musculoskeletal system.

- **Code set:** 20100–29999

- All arthroscopic procedures and codes used to report procedures on bone marrow are excluded from the musculoskeletal system code set.

Respiratory System
- The respiratory system is responsible for carrying oxygen throughout the body and expels carbon dioxide.

- **Code set:** 30000–32999

Cardiovascular System

- The cardiovascular system comprises the capillaries, veins, venules, arteries, and heart.

- **Code set:** 33016–37799

Hemic and Lymphatic Systems

- The spleen, bone marrow, stem cells, and lymph nodes are part of the hemic and lymphatic systems.

- **Code set:** 38100–38999

- **Surgical procedures on spleen:** 38100–38200

- **General surgical procedures:** 38204–38232

- **Transplantation and post-transplantation cellular infusions:** 38240–38243

- **Surgical procedures on lymph nodes and lymphatic channels:** 38300–38999

Digestive System

- The digestive system is in charge of food intake, digestion, and assimilation, as well as the disposal of residual digestive waste products.

- **Code set:** 40490–49999

Urinary System

- The kidneys, ureters, urinary bladder, and urethra comprise the urinary system.

- **Code set:** 50010–53899

Reproductive System

- The prostate, testes, seminal vesicles, vas deferens, and penis comprise the male genital system. The uterus, ovaries, fallopian tubes, cervix, and vagina comprise the female genital system.

- **Code set:** 55920-55920

Endocrine System
- The endocrine system is responsible for the hormones of the body.
- **Code set:** 60000–60699

Nervous System
- The nervous system is made up of two parts: the central nervous system and the peripheral nervous system. The central nervous system is the body's control center, and the peripheral nervous system consists of the cranial and spinal nerves.
- **Code set:** 61000–64999

Eye and Ear
- **Code set:** 65091–69979

CHAPTER 3:

EVALUATION AND MANAGEMENT (E/M)

Choose the codes that best reflect the services provided during the visit. Particular medical necessity standards in statutes, regulations, and manuals, as well as specific medical necessity criteria outlined by National Coverage Determinations and Local Coverage Determinations, must be met by services. For each service billed, you must specify the exact sign, symptom, or patient complaint that justifies and necessitates the service (American Medical Association, 2022).

The HCPCS is a code set that is compliant with the Health Insurance Portability and Accountability Act and is used by providers to report procedures, services, medications, and equipment given by physicians and other non-physician practitioners, hospital outpatient facilities, ambulatory surgical centers, and other outpatient facilities. CPT codes are included in this system (American Medical Association, 2022).

The ICD-10-CM code set is used by physicians to report medical diagnoses on all sorts of claims for services rendered in the United States. ICD-10-PCS is a code set used by facilities to report inpatient treatments and services provided in hospital inpatient health care settings in the United States. Use HCPCS codes to report ambulatory and physician services, including those provided during an inpatient hospitalization (American Medical Association, 2022).

When picking the code that best describes the service provided, the following factors must be considered: patient type, setting of service, and level of E/M service performed.

3.1 Places of Services

E/M services are separated into different settings based on where they are provided. Examples of settings include:

- Office or other outpatient setting

- Hospital inpatient

- Emergency department

- Nursing facility (American Medical Association, 2022)

3.2 Patient Type

Patients are classified as either new or established for billing purposes for E/M services based on previous encounters with the provider. A new patient is a person who has not previously received professional services from the physician/non-physician practitioner (NPP) or another physician of the same specialty who belongs to the same group practice within the previous three years. An established patient is someone who has received professional treatment from the physician/NPP or another physician of the same specialty from the same group practice within the last three years (American Medical Association, 2022).

3.3 Level of E/M Service Performed

Various categories and levels are used to arrange the code sets used to bill for E/M services. Generally speaking, the higher level of code you may bill within the relevant category depends on how complex the visit was. To bill any code, the services provided must meet the code's definition. You must ensure that the codes chosen properly represent the services provided. History, examination, and medical decision-making are the three most important factors in determining the appropriate level of E/M services delivered. Visits that are primarily focused on counseling and/or care coordination are an exception to this guideline. Time is the most important aspect in qualifying for a specific level of E/M services during these visits (American Medical Association, 2022).

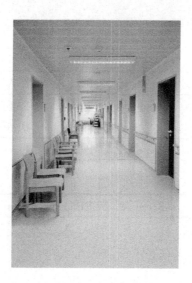

Elements Required for Each Type of History

The table below displays the elements needed for each type of history. To be eligible for a specific type of history, all four elements listed in the row must be met. It is worth mentioning that as the intensity of the history increases, so do the ingredients required to conduct that history. A problem-focused history, for example, includes documentation of the chief complaint (CC) and a brief history of present illness (HPI). Whereas a detailed history requires documentation of a CC, an extended HPI, an extended review of systems (ROS), and relevant past, family, and/or social history (PFSH). While the CC must be documented at all levels, the amount of information gathered for the remaining elements connected to a patient's history is determined by clinical judgment and the nature of the presenting problem (American Medical Association, 2022).

Table 1.

Type of History	CC	HPI	ROS	PFSH
Problem-Focused	Required	Brief	N/A	N/A
Expanded Problem-Focused	Required	Brief	Problem-Pertinent	N/A
Detailed	Required	Extended	Extended	Pertinent
Comprehensive	Required	Extended	Complete	Complete

Chief Complaint (CC)

A CC is a brief statement that outlines the symptom, problem, condition, diagnosis, or purpose for the patient's visit. Typically, the CC is stated in the patient's words. For example, a patient may complain of stomach pain, aching joints, and exhaustion. The CC should be clearly documented in the medical record (American Medical Association, 2022).

History of Present Illness (HPI)

HPI is a chronological account of the progression of the patient's current illness from the earliest sign and/or symptom to the present. HPI components include:

- Location (example: left leg)

- Quality (example: aching, burning, radiating pain)

- Severity (example: 10 on a scale of 1 to 10)

- Duration (example: started 3 days ago)

- Timing (example: constant or comes and goes)

- Context (example: lifted large object at work)

- Modifying factors (example: better when heat is applied)

- Associated signs and symptoms (example: numbness in toes) (American Medical Association, 2022)

HPIs are classified into two types: brief and extended. One to three HPI elements are documented in a brief HPI. Three HPI aspects are documented in this example: location, quality, and duration.

- CC: The patient complains of ear pain

- Brief HPI: A dull pain in the left ear over the past 24 hours (American Medical Association, 2022)

An expanded HPI adheres to documentation criteria established in 1995 and should describe four or more components of the current HPI or associated comorbidities. Alternatively, the 1997 documentation criteria require at least four aspects of the current HPI or the state of at least three chronic or inactive conditions. To document an E/M service provided on or after September 10, 2013, you may utilize the 1997 documentation guidelines for an extended HPI along with other components from the 1995 documentation guidelines (American Medical Association, 2022).

In this example, five HPI elements are documented: location, quality, duration, and modifying factors.

- CC: The patient complains of ear pain

- Extended HPI: The patient has complained of a dull ache in his left ear for the past 24 hours. The patient claims to have gone swimming two days ago. Warm compresses and ibuprofen helped to alleviate symptoms (American Medical Association, 2022).

Review of Systems (ROS)

ROS is a bodily system inventory gathered through a series of questions designed to detect signs and/or symptoms that the patient may be experiencing or has experienced. These systems are appropriate for ROS purposes:

- Constitutional Symptoms (for example, fever, weight loss)

- Eyes

- Ears, nose, mouth, throat

- Cardiovascular

- Respiratory

- Gastrointestinal

- Genitourinary

- Musculoskeletal

- Integumentary (skin and/or breast)

- Neurological

- Psychiatric

- Endocrine

- Hematologic/lymphatic

- Allergic/immunologic (American Medical Association, 2022)

The three types of ROS are problem-pertinent, extended, and complete. A problem pertinent ROS questions the system that is directly related to the HPI problem. In this example, one system, the ear, is examined:

- CC: Earache

- ROS: Positive for pain in the left ear. Denies experiencing dizziness, tinnitus, fullness, or headache (American Medical Association, 2022)

An extended ROS inquires about the system directly connected to the problem(s) identified in the HPI, as well as a restricted number of additional systems (two to nine).

- CC: In-office follow-up following cardiac catheterization. "I feel terrific," the patient says

- ROS: The patient claims to be in good health and denies any chest pain, syncope, palpitations, or shortness of breath. Relates to sporadic unilateral, asymptomatic edema of the left leg (American Medical Association, 2022)

A complete ROS investigates the system(s) directly connected to the problem(s) indicated in the HPI, as well as all additional (minimum of 10) organ systems. Individual documentation of those systems with positive or pertinent negative reactions is required. A notation stating that all other systems are negative is permissible for the remaining systems. In the absence of such a notation, you must document at least ten systems individually (American Medical Association, 2022).

In this case, ten signs and symptoms are examined:

- CC: Patient complains of "fainting spell"

- ROS:

    - Constitutional: Weight stable, + fatigue

    - Eyes: + loss of peripheral vision

    - Ear, nose, mouth, throat: No complaints

    - Cardiovascular: + palpitations; denies chest pain; denies calf pain, pressure, or edema.

- Respiratory: + shortness of breath on exertion

- Gastrointestinal: Appetite good, denies heartburn and indigestion. + episodes of nausea. Bowel movement daily; denies constipation or loose stools

- Urinary: Denies incontinence, frequency, urgency, nocturia, pain, or discomfort

- Skin: + clammy, moist skin

- Neurological: + fainting; denies numbness, tingling, and tremors

- Psychiatric: Denies memory loss or depression. Mood pleasant (American Medical Association, 2022)

Past, Family, and/or Social History (PFSH)

PFSH is a review of one's previous history, including illnesses, operations, injuries, and treatments. In addition, a review of medical events, diseases, and inherited conditions may put the patient at risk, as well as a social history that includes an age-appropriate examination of previous and current events (American Medical Association, 2022).

The two types of PFSH are both pertinent and complete. A pertinent PFSH is an assessment of the historical areas that are directly related to the HPI problem(s). In the pertinent PFSH, at least one item from each of the three history sections must be documented (American Medical Association, 2022).

In this case, the patient's prior surgical history is examined in relation to the identified HPI:

- HPI: Coronary artery disease

- PFSH: Patient returns to office for follow-up of coronary artery bypass graft in 1992. Recent cardiac catheterization demonstrates 50% occlusion of vein graft to the obtuse marginal artery (American Medical Association, 2022)

A complete PFSH is an evaluation of two or all three areas, depending on the type of E/M service. A complete PFSH needs a review of all three history sections for services that, by definition, comprise a comprehensive assessment or reassessment of the patient. For other services, a review of two historical areas is adequate (American Medical Association, 2022).

For a complete PFSH for these categories of E/M services, you must document at least one specific item from two of the three history areas:

- Office or other outpatient services, established patient

- Emergency department

- Domiciliary care, established patient

- Subsequent nursing facility care (if following the 1995 documentation guidelines)

- Home care, established patient (American Medical Association, 2022)

For each of the following categories of E/M services, you must document at least one specific item from each of the history areas:

- Office or other outpatient services, new patient

- Hospital observation services

- Hospital inpatient services, initial care

- Consultations

- Comprehensive nursing facility assessments

- Domiciliary care, new patient

- Home care, new patient (American Medical Association, 2022)

In this case, the patient's genetic history is evaluated in relation to the present HPI:

- HPI: Coronary artery disease

- PFSH: Family history reveals:

- Maternal grandparents – Both + for coronary artery disease; grandfather: deceased at age 69; grandmother: still living

- Paternal grandparents – Grandmother: + diabetes, hypertension; grandfather: + heart attack at age 55

- Parents: – Mother: + obesity, diabetes; father: + heart attack at age 51. Deceased at age 57 of heart attack

- Siblings – Sister: + diabetes, obesity, hypertension, age 39; brother: + heart attack at age 45, living (American Medical Association, 2022)

Notes on the Documentation of History and Exam

To simplify history and exam documentation for established patients for office/outpatient visits, practitioners may choose to focus their documentation on what has changed since the last visit, or on pertinent items that have not changed, and need not re-record the defined list of required elements if there is evidence that the practitioner reviewed the previous information and updated it as needed (American Medical Association, 2022).

The billing practitioner may evaluate the material, amend it, or augment it as necessary, and indicate in the medical record that he or she has done so rather than having to re-document any aspect of the principal complaint or history that has already been recorded in the medical record by ancillary staff or the beneficiary. You can include the CC, ROS, and PFSH as independent elements of history or as part of the HPI description (American Medical Association, 2022).

You don't need to record the ROS and/or PFSH obtained at an earlier session again if there is evidence that the physician reviewed and revised the earlier data. This might happen when a doctor changes his or her personal record, or in an institutional environment or group practice where multiple doctors use the same record. You can document the review and update by explaining any new ROS and/or PFSH information or noting that there has been no change in the information, as well as identifying the date and location of the last ROS and/or PFSH (American Medical Association, 2022).

Ancillary personnel may keep track of the HPI, ROS, and/or PFSH. In addition, the patient may fill out a form to provide the ROS and/or PFSH. You must provide a notation complementing or confirming the information provided by others to demonstrate that the physician reviewed the information. If the physician is unable to collect a history from the patient or another source, the record should reflect the patient's condition or another factor that prevents the physician from obtaining a history (American Medical Association, 2022).

Examination

The most significant differences between the 1995 and 1997 editions of the documentation guidelines occur in the section on examination documentation. For a patient encounter, while billing Medicare, you may utilize any version but not both of the documentation guidelines. To document an E/M service provided on or after September 10, 2013, you may utilize the 1997 documentation guidelines for an extended HPI along with other features from the

1995 documentation guidelines (American Medical Association, 2022).

Levels of E/M services are based on four types of examination:

1. **Problem-focused:** A limited assessment of the organ system or bodily area in question

2. **Expanded Problem-Focused:** A restricted evaluation of the affected body area or organ system, as well as any other symptomatic or connected body location(s) or organ system

3. **Detailed:** An extensive evaluation of the damaged body parts or organ systems, as well as any symptomatic or connected body parts or organ systems

4. **Comprehensive**: A general multi-system examination or complete examination of a single organ system and other symptomatic or related body areas or organ systems under the 1997 documentation guidelines (American Medical Association, 2022)

An examination may encompass multiple organ systems or just one. The nature and extent of the examination are influenced by clinical judgment, patient history, and the nature of the presenting problem(s). The 1997 documentation standards distinguish two types of comprehensive tests that can be performed during a patient visit: general multi-system evaluation and single organ examination. The assessment of one or more organ systems or body locations is part of a general multi-system examination (American Medical Association, 2022).

Table 2.

Type of Examination	Description
Problem-Focused	Includes performance and documentation of one to five bullet-pointed items in one or more organ systems or body areas.
Expanded Problem-Focused	In one or more organ system(s) or body area(s), includes performance and documentation of at least six elements denoted by a bullet(s).
Detailed	At least six organ systems or bodily locations should be included. Performance and documentation of at least two components marked by a bullet are expected for each system/area chosen. Alternatively, at least 12 bullet-pointed items must be performed and documented in at least two or more organ systems or bodily regions.
Comprehensive	At least nine organ systems or bodily locations should be included. All parts of the examination listed by a bullet should be performed for each system/area selected unless explicit guidelines limit the content of the examination. Documentation of at least two items indicated by a bullet is expected for each area/system (American Medical Association, 2022).*

*According to the 1995 documentation guidelines, the medical record for a basic multi-system assessment should include findings from at least eight organ systems (American Medical Association, 2022).

A single organ system examination entails a more thorough evaluation of a single organ system.

Table 3.

Type of Examination	Description
Problem-Focused	Includes performance and documentation for one to five components indicated by a bullet in a box with a shaded or unshaded outline.
Expanded Problem-Focused	In a box with either a shaded or an unshaded border, includes performance and documentation of at least six elements specified by a bullet.
Detailed	All other tests, with the exception of eye and psychiatric assessments, should include the execution and documentation of at least 12 items indicated with a bullet, either in a box with a shaded or unshaded border. Eye and psychiatric tests include the execution and documentation of at least nine items identified with a bullet point, be it in a box with a shaded or unshaded border.
Comprehensive	Includes all elements that are specified in a bullet, whether they are in a box that is shaded or not. Every element in each box with a shaded border and at least one element in each box with an unshaded border is expected to be documented (American Medical Association, 2022).

Both types of examinations can be performed by any physician, regardless of specialty.

When documenting generic multi-system and single organ system assessments (in both the 1995 and 1997 documentation guidelines), keep the following points in mind:

- The evaluation of the diseased or symptomatic bodily area(s) or organ system(s) should produce specific aberrant and significant negative results and should be documented. A simple indication of "abnormal" without any explanation is insufficient.

- Describe any abnormal or unexpected findings from any asymptomatic bodily area(s) or organ system(s) testing.

- To document normal findings linked to unaffected area(s) or asymptomatic organ system(s), a simple statement or description indicating "negative" or "normal" is adequate (American Medical Association, 2022).

Medical Decision-Making

The complexity of establishing a diagnosis and/or selecting a management option is determined by taking the following elements into account:

- The number of potential diagnoses and/or management choices that must be considered

- The amount and/or complexity of medical records, diagnostic tests, and/or other information that must be acquired, reviewed, and analyzed

- The possibility of substantial complications, morbidity, and/or death, as well as comorbidities related to the patient's presenting problem(s), diagnostic procedure(s), and/or possible management options (American Medical Association, 2022)

The table below shows how the elements required for each stage of medical decision-making progress. It should be noted that in order to qualify for a specific form of medical decision-making, two or three elements must be met or exceeded.

Table 4.

CPT Codes	Type of Decision-Making	Number of Diagnoses or Management Options	Amount and/or Complexity of Data to be Reviewed	Risk of Significant Complications, Morbidity, and/or Mortality
99202, 99212	Straightforward	Minimal	Minimal or None	Minimal
99203, 99213	Low	Limited	Limited	Low
99204, 99214	Moderate	Multiple	Moderate	Moderate
99205, 99215	High	Extensive	Extensive	High

(American Medical Association, 2022)

Number of Diagnoses and/or Management Options

The quantity and nature of the problems addressed during the encounter, the difficulty of making a diagnosis, and the doctor's management decisions all affect the number of potential diagnoses and/or treatment choices to take into account (American Medical Association, 2022).

In general, making a decision about a diagnosed problem is easier than making a decision about a recognized but undiagnosed problem. The number of probable diagnoses may be indicated by the number and type of diagnostic tests conducted. Less troublesome than issues that are deteriorating or not changing as expected are issues that are improving, or finding solutions. The need to seek guidance from other healthcare specialists is another indicator of the intricacy of diagnostic or management problems (American Medical Association, 2022).

Several crucial considerations when recording the number of diagnoses or treatment choices: a diagnosis, clinical impression, or assessment should be included for each contact. These elements may be explicitly stated or inferred from written judgments about management strategies and/or additional testing. This is for a presenting problem with a confirmed diagnosis; the documentation should state if the issue is better, under good management, resolving, or resolved; or whether it is inadequately controlled, worsening, or failing to change as expected. When a presenting problem does not have an established diagnosis, the assessment or clinical impression may be given in the form of differential diagnoses or as a "possible," "probable," or "rule out" diagnosis (American Medical Association, 2022).

You should also document the start of, or changes to, treatment, including a variety of management alternatives such as patient directions, nursing instructions, therapies, and medication. Also, if referrals are made, consultations are requested, or advice is sought, who makes the referral, where the consultation is requested, and from whom counsel is sought (American Medical Association, 2022).

Amount and/or Complexity of Data to be Reviewed

The amount and/or complexity of data to be evaluated is determined by the type of diagnostic testing ordered or reviewed. A decision to obtain and review old medical records and/or obtain a history from sources other than the patient (increases the amount and complexity of data to be reviewed), a discussion of contradictory or unexpected test results with the physician who performed or interpreted the test (indicates the complexity of data to be reviewed), and the physician who ordered a test personally reviewing the images are all indicators of the amount and complexity of data to be reviewed (indicates the complexity of data to be reviewed) (American Medical Association, 2022).

Important points:

- You should record the type of service if a diagnostic procedure is ordered, planned, scheduled, or carried out during the E/M contact.

- Laboratory, radiology, and/or other diagnostic tests are reviewed. It is sufficient to write "WBC elevated" or "Chest x-ray unremarkable." Alternatively, you can document the review by starting and dating a report that includes the test findings.

- A decision to acquire old documents or additional history from the patient's family, caregiver, or another source in order to supplement information obtained from the patient.

- Relevant results from a study of old data and/or additional information from the patient's relatives, caregiver, or another source to supplement information gathered from the patient as applicable, you should document that there is no additional relevant information beyond what has already been received. A simple remark of "Old records reviewed" or "Additional history gathered from family" is insufficient.

- Discussion with the physician who performed or evaluated the study regarding the results of laboratory, radiology, or other diagnostic tests.

- The independent visualization and interpretation of an image, tracing, or specimen that has previously or subsequently been interpreted by another physician (American Medical Association, 2022).

Risk of Significant Complications, Morbidity, and/or Mortality

The risks associated with the following categories: presenting problem(s), diagnostic procedure(s), and possible management options determine the risk of major complications, morbidity, and/or fatality. The risk of the presenting problem(s) is assessed based on the risk of the disease process anticipated between the current encounter and the future encounter. The risk of choosing diagnostic methods and management alternatives is based on the risk during and shortly after any procedure or treatment. The overall risk is determined by the maximum level of risk in any one category. The risk of significant complications, morbidity, and/or mortality can be minimal, low, moderate, or high (American Medical Association, 2022).

Some important points to remember when documenting the risk levels: Comorbidities/underlying diseases or other conditions that complicate medical decision-making by increasing the chance of complications, morbidity, and/or mortality should be noted. At the time of the E/M contact, if a surgical or invasive diagnostic procedure is ordered, planned, or scheduled, it should be noted along with the kind of surgery. If a surgical or invasive diagnostic procedure is conducted at the time of the E/M encounter, it should be listed alongside the specific operation. And document the referral for or decision to perform an urgent surgical or invasive diagnostic treatment (American Medical Association, 2022).

Documentation of an Encounter Dominated by Counseling and/or Coordination of Care

Time is regarded as the primary or governing criterion in establishing eligibility for a certain level of E/M services when counseling and/or care coordination dominate (more than 50% of) the physician/patient and/or family contact (face-to-face time in the office or other outpatient setting, floor/unit time in the hospital or nursing facility).If the level of service is based on counseling and/or care coordination, you should document the overall length of the interaction and the record should detail the counseling and/or care coordination activities (American Medical Association, 2022).

The American Medical Association's Level I and Level II CPT books include average time guidelines for a range of E/M treatments. This includes work completed before, during, and after the interaction. The times specified in the code descriptors are averages and so represent a range of times that may be higher or lower depending on actual medical situations (American Medical Association, 2022).

Other Considerations

Consultation Services

Beginning on or after January 1, 2010, Medicare no longer accepts inpatient consultation codes (CPT codes 99251–99255) and office as well as other outpatient consultation codes (CPT codes 99241–99245) for Part B payment purposes. Medicare will cover telehealth consultation codes (HCPCS G0406–G0408 and G0425–G0427). Physicians and NPPs who provide services that would have been reported as CPT consultation codes prior to January 1, 2010, should record the appropriate E/M visit code to bill for these services commencing January 1, 2010 (American Medical Association, 2022).

Formative Assessment Questions:

1. What is the difference between the ICD-10-CM and ICD-10-PCS code sets?

2. Why is endoscopy a common surgical method for diagnostic and therapeutic treatments?
3. History, examination, and medical decision-making are the three most important factors in determining the appropriate level of E/M services delivered. What is the one exception to this guideline?
4. How does the physician decide on the level of complexity when establishing a diagnosis or choosing a management option?

Key Concepts

- The **HCPCS** is a code set compliant with the Health Insurance Portability and Accountability Act.

- The **ICD-10-CM** code set is used by physicians to report medical diagnoses on all sorts of claims for services rendered in the United States.

- **ICD-10-PCS** is a code set used by facilities to report inpatient treatments and services provided in hospital inpatient health care settings in the United States.

- Patients are classified as either new or established for billing purposes for E/M services based on previous encounters with the provider.

- Each type of history needs all four elements as listed:

  - **Chief complaint (CC):** a brief statement that outlines the symptom, problem, condition, diagnosis, or purpose for the patient's visit

  - **History of present illness (HPI):** a chronological account of the progression of the patient's current illness from the earliest sign and/or symptom to the present

  - **Review of systems (ROS):** a bodily system inventory gathered through a series of questions designed to detect signs and/or symptoms that the patient may be experiencing or has experienced

  - **Past, family, and/or social history (PFSH):** a review of one's previous history, including illnesses, operations, injuries, and treatments

- To simplify history and exam documentation for established patients for office/outpatient visits, practitioners may choose to focus their documentation on what has changed since the last visit or on pertinent items that have not changed.

- Levels of E/M services are based on four types of examination: **problem-focused, expanded problem-focused, detailed, comprehensive.**

- The quantity and nature of the problems addressed during the encounter, the difficulty of making a diagnosis, and the doctor's management decisions all affect the number of potential diagnoses and/or treatment choices to take into account.

- The amount and/or complexity of data to be evaluated is determined by the type of diagnostic testing ordered or reviewed.

- Comorbidities/underlying diseases or other conditions that complicate medical decision-making by increasing the chance of complications, morbidity, and/or mortality should be noted.

- Time is regarded as the primary or governing criterion in establishing eligibility for a certain level of E/M services.

CHAPTER 4:

ANESTHESIA

You won't experience pain during surgery, medical procedures, or examinations because of breakthroughs in medicine and anesthetics. However, surgery and anesthesia are inherently dangerous, so understanding what anesthesia is, how different types work, and how to avoid potential risks is vital (American Society of Anesthesiologists, 2022a).

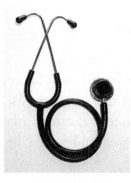

4.1 Types of Anesthesia

During surgery, medical procedures, or examinations, many types of anesthesia are used to keep you comfortable and pain-free. However, there are some significant differences. The type you receive will be determined by the surgery, your health, and your personal preferences (American Society of Anesthesiologists, 2022a).

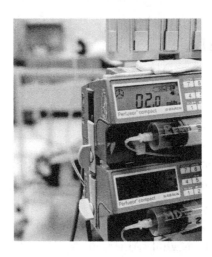

General Anesthesia

Although there are many different types and levels of anesthesia, general anesthesia is frequently used for major surgeries, including heart surgery, knee and hip replacements, and numerous surgical procedures for the treatment of cancer. Many of these surgeries are life-saving or life-changing and would be impossible to perform without general anesthesia (American Society of Anesthesiologists, 2022d).

How does it work?

A physician anesthesiologist will deliver general anesthesia through a mask or an IV inserted into a vein. The patient will be unconscious while the anesthetic is operating, and many of their body's functions will slow down or require assistance to function properly. To help the patient breathe, a tube may be put in the throat. The medical anesthesiologist will monitor the patient's heart rate, blood pressure, breathing, and other vital signs during surgery or the operation to ensure they are normal and steady while the patient is unconscious and pain-free (American Society of Anesthesiologists, 2022d).

After the surgery, the physician anesthesiologist will reverse the drug and monitor the patient's respiration, circulation, and oxygen levels while they return to consciousness. Some patients wake up feeling good, while others endure symptoms such as nausea, vomiting, chills, or a sore throat as a result of the breathing tube. These symptoms will be managed by the physician anesthesiologist (American Society of Anesthesiologists, 2022d).

As a result of the surgery, the patient will most likely have pain and discomfort as they recuperate, which may worsen as the effects of the general anesthesia wear off. The patient will be advised by the physician anesthesiologist on how to control their pain while recovering in the hospital and at home. If the patient is able to leave the hospital on the day of the surgery, they will be unable to drive after undergoing general anesthesia. The anesthesia medicine may take a day or two to completely leave the body, which will influence the patient's judgment, reflexes, and sleepiness (American Society of Anesthesiologists, 2022d).

IV/Monitored Sedation

Sedation

Physicians now have numerous options for making their patients as comfortable as possible during surgery or treatments for identifying medical disorders. Sedation is a common sort of pain control that relaxes you and sometimes causes you to fall asleep. Sedation, also known as monitored anesthesia care, or conscious sedation, is commonly used for minor surgeries or shorter, less complicated procedures when a local anesthetic injection isn't enough but deeper general anesthesia isn't required. Some of these procedures may entail biopsies or the use of a scope to check the throat or colon in order to detect and treat medical conditions such as cancer (American Society of Anesthesiologists, 2022e).

Sedation is typically administered via an IV inserted into a vein. Sedation levels might vary from minimal to deep depending on the operation. Sedation, whether moderate or deep, may cause the patient's breathing to slow down, and they may be given oxygen in some circumstances. Even with deep sedation, the patient will not be unconscious, as with general anesthesia. When the surgery is finished and the medicines are stopped, most patients awaken quickly. Possible side effects include headaches, nausea, and some drowsiness, but patients will likely experience fewer problems than with general anesthesia and they will most likely recover faster and return home sooner. IV sedation is sometimes used in conjunction with other types of pain relief, such as local anesthesia, which requires one or more injections to numb a small part of the body, or regional anesthesia, which numbs a greater area of the body, such as from the waist down (American Society of Anesthesiologists, 2022e).

Levels of Sedation

- Minimal sedation will help patients relax but they will most likely remain conscious. They'll comprehend the doctor's queries and be able to respond as well as follow orders. This level of sedation is usually used when the doctor requires the patient to be present during the treatment.

- Moderate — During the operation, patients will feel tired and may possibly fall asleep. Patients may or may not recall some of the procedure.

- Deep — The patient will not be completely unconscious but they will sleep through the operation and have little or no recall of it (American Society of Anesthesiologists, 2022e).

Regional Anesthesia

Regional anesthesia, as previously stated, is a method of pain management for surgery that numbs a large portion of the body, such as from the waist down. The medication is administered through injection or a small tube known as a catheter and is used when a simple injection of local anesthetic is insufficient and it is ideal for the patient to be awake (American Society of Anesthesiologists, 2022g).

This type of anesthetic, which includes spinal blocks and epidurals, is frequently used during labor. In fact, epidurals are the most common type of pain relief given during labor and delivery. It alleviates labor pain while allowing the mother to remain aware. A stronger spinal block is employed during procedures such as cesarean deliveries, generally known as C-sections (American Society of Anesthesiologists, 2022g).

Spinal blocks and epidurals allow the doctor to deliver the baby surgically without causing pain to the mother or introducing the newborn to potentially hazardous sedative substances. Regional anesthesia is quite safe and does not have the possible risks and side effects that sedation and general anesthesia do. It does, however, pose some hazards, and it is critical that it be administered and supervised by a physician anesthesiologist (American Society of Anesthesiologists, 2022g).

Local Anesthesia

Local anesthesia, also known as local anesthetic, is a single injection of medication that numbs a small area of the body. It's used for things like performing a skin or breast biopsy, mending a fractured bone, or stitching a deep wound. You will be awake and attentive, and you may feel pressure, but no pain on the site being treated. Side effects and risks from local anesthetic are uncommon and typically minimal. You may, for example, feel some soreness where the medication was injected. In rare situations, the anesthesia may cause an allergic reaction (American Society of Anesthesiologists, 2022f).

Some treatments cannot be performed without the use of general anesthesia or sedation. However, for many procedures, the doctor will suggest a local anesthetic. In some cases, the patient may have an alternative choice. If they do not want to be sedated, ask the surgeon or physician anesthesiologist if the surgery may be done safely and comfortably with a local anesthetic. Patients will not only recover faster and return home sooner but the operation may also be less expensive. Local anesthesia is sometimes used with sedation (American Society of Anesthesiologists, 2022f).

4.2 Effects of Anesthesia

If you're under general anesthesia, a medical anesthesiologist should monitor you before and after the operation to manage any side effects and keep an eye out for more serious concerns (American Society of Anesthesiologists, 2022c).

General anesthesia can have the following side effects:

- Nausea and vomiting: The most common negative effects are nausea and vomiting. These can happen in the initial few hours or days following surgery and are caused by medicine, motion, and the type of procedure.

- Sore throat: The tube placed in the throat can leave the patient with a sore throat once it is removed.

- Postoperative delirium: Confusion when recovering consciousness after surgery is normal but for some people, especially elderly patients, the confusion can last for up to a week. They may feel disoriented and have difficulty remembering or concentrating.

- Muscle aches: Soreness can be caused by the medicines used to relax the muscles so that a breathing tube can be inserted.

- Itching: This is a frequent side effect of narcotics, a type of pain medication that is occasionally used in conjunction with general anesthesia.

- Chills and shivering (hypothermia): This happens to up to half of all patients when they regain consciousness following surgery and it could be related to body temperature (American Society of Anesthesiologists, 2022c).

More serious complications include:

- Postoperative delirium or cognitive dysfunction: Confusion and memory loss might last for many hours or days in rare circumstances. Certain patients may experience long-term memory and learning impairments as a result of a condition known as postoperative cognitive dysfunction.

- Malignant hypothermia: Some people inherit this dangerous, sometimes fatal, reaction to anesthesia that can develop during surgery, triggering rapid fever and muscle contractions (American Society of Anesthesiologists, 2022c).

Sedation has fewer possible side effects than general anesthetics, including headache, nausea, and drowsiness. These adverse effects are usually temporary. Because sedation levels vary, it is critical to be monitored during surgery to ensure patients do not have any issues.

- Headache: This might happen a few days after surgery if some spinal fluid seeps out when regional anesthesia is administered through the spine, such as during a childbirth epidural or spinal block.

- Minor back pain: Soreness at the site of injection in the back.

- Difficulty urinating: If the patients were numbed from the waist down, urinating may be difficult for a short time following the procedure.

- Hematoma: Bleeding underneath the skin can happen at the site of the anesthetic injection (American Society of Anesthesiologists, 2022c).

The following are rare but serious complications:

- Pneumothorax: When anesthesia is injected near the lungs, the needle could enter the lung by accident. This could cause the lung to collapse, requiring the insertion of a chest tube to reinflate the lung.

- Nerve damage: Although nerve damage is extremely rare, it can occur and cause temporary or permanent pain (American Society of Anesthesiologists, 2022c).

Local anesthesia has the lowest risk of adverse effects, and any that do occur are usually minimal. Patients may feel sore or itchy where the medication was injected. Additionally, **regional anesthesia** does not have the potential complications and side effects that can occur with sedation and general anesthesia. However, it does carry some risks (American Society of Anesthesiologists, 2022c).

4.3 Factors That Increase Risk With Anesthesia

Certain people are more likely to experience problems or complications, and possibly even death, due to their age, medical conditions, or the type of surgery they are undergoing. If a patient has any of the following conditions now or in the past, the risk with anesthesia could be higher:

- A history of negative reactions to anesthesia or allergies
- Diabetes
- Heart disease, including angina, valve disease, heart failure, or a previous heart attack
- High blood pressure
- Kidney issues
- Lung conditions, like asthma or chronic obstructive pulmonary disease (COPD)
- Obesity
- Obstructive sleep apnea
- Stroke
- Seizures or other neurological disorders
- Smoking, or drinking more than two alcoholic beverages per day also increases the risk (American Society of Anesthesiologists, 2022b)

Formative Assessment Questions:

1. Why does the left ventricle have the largest and strongest muscles?

2. What is the purpose of cerebrospinal fluid?

3. How are E/M services separated?

4. Why would a patient be unable to drive after undergoing general anesthesia?

5. If a patient undergoes sedation, in a rare complication, why would their lung need to be reinflated?

6. How is a doctor able to deliver a baby without causing pain to the mother or potentially harming the newborn?

Key Concepts

Types of anesthesia are as follows:

- **General anesthesia**: A state of controlled sleep using a mask or IV, Mostly used for surgeries considered life-saving or life-changing (like major surgeries, including heart surgery, knee and hip replacements, and numerous surgical procedures for the treatment of cancer).

- **IV/Monitored sedation:** A common sort of pain control that relaxes you and sometimes causes you to fall asleep. This is administered via an IV. Typical for minor or less complicated procedures.

  - Minimal

  - Moderate

  - Deep

- **Regional anesthesia:** A method of pain management for surgery that numbs a large portion of the body, such as from the waist down. Administered through injection or a catheter. Frequently used during labor.

- **Local anesthesia:** A single injection of medication that numbs a small area of the body. Used for things like performing a skin or breast biopsy, mending a fractured bone, or stitching a deep wound.

Side effects of anesthesia include:

- **General anesthesia**

  - Nausea and vomiting

  - Sore throat

  - Postoperative delirium

- Muscle aches
- Itching
- Chills and shivering
- Malignant hypothermia
- **Sedation**
  - Headache
  - Minor back pain
  - Difficulty urinating
  - Hematoma
  - Pneumothorax
  - Nerve damage
- **Local anesthesia**
  - Itchiness or soreness where anesthesia was injected

CHAPTER 5:

RADIOLOGY

Radiology is a series of tests that take pictures or create images of various body parts. It is often referred to as diagnostic imaging. The field is divided into two branches: diagnostic radiology and interventional radiology, both of which use radiant energy to detect and treat diseases. While there are several imaging exams, some of the most popular are X-rays, MRIs, ultrasounds, CT scans, and PET scans (Health Images, 2020).

5.1 Diagnostic Radiology

Diagnostic radiology is a medical specialty that entails performing a variety of imaging procedures in order to gather images of the inside of the body. The diagnostic radiologist then meticulously analyses these images in order to determine illness and injury. In modern medicine, diagnostic radiology is at the center of clinical decision-making (Inside Radiology, 2016a).

Diagnostic imaging tests involve:

- X-rays (plain radiography)
- CT (computed tomography) scans
- MRI (magnetic resonance imaging) scans
- Ultrasound examinations (also known as sonography)
- Nuclear medicine imaging techniques (Inside Radiology, 2016a)

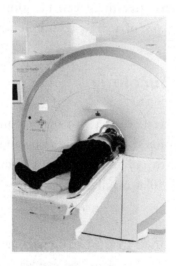

5.2 Interventional Radiology

In order to gather images of the inside of the body, interventional radiology, a medical speciality, uses a range of imaging techniques. The interventional radiologist analyses these images carefully in order to identify injury and disease and to conduct a variety of interventional medical procedures. Imaging techniques used by interventional radiologists include X-rays, MRIs, fluoroscopy (an How do you define diagnostic radiology? X-ray treatment that allows physicians to observe internal organs in motion), CT scans, and ultrasounds (Inside Radiology, 2018).

Interventional radiologists treat tumors, perform organ biopsies, and place stents by inserting tiny instruments and catheters into the body through an artery or vein. The images are used to direct catheters and devices to the precise location of the procedure or treatment. This eliminates the need for traditional (open) or keyhole (laparoscopic) surgery because treatment can be administered by using a small plastic tube the size of a straw (Inside Radiology, 2018).

5.3 Radiation Oncology

Radiation oncology treats cancer and many non-malignant diseases with radiation (radiation therapy). It is a safe and effective treatment for many cancers, with radiation therapy playing a role in the successful treatment of 40% of all cancer patients worldwide (Inside Radiology, 2016b).

Radiation therapy is used to treat malignancies located everywhere in the body. It destroys or damages cancer cells, inhibiting their growth, multiplication, and spread. Cancerous cells are more sensitive to radiation than healthy cells. In treatment, several types of high-energy radiation are used, including: high-energy X-rays, electron beams, and gamma rays (Inside Radiology, 2016b).

5.4 Types of Imaging

Abdominal Imaging

Abdominal imaging is a diagnostic radiology specialty that entails imaging the abdomen and pelvis, which includes the genitals, urinary organs, and gastrointestinal tract, in order to diagnose and plan medical treatment.

Imaging is used by abdominal imaging radiologists to diagnose diseases of the liver, bladder, and kidneys; prostate and uterus, pancreas, colon, and gallbladder, as well as adrenal glands. Abdominal imaging studies include CT colonography, MRI enterography or enteroclysis, MRI scan of the rectum, MRI of the prostate, and transarterial chemoembolization (TACE) (Inside Radiology, 2017).

Breast Imaging

Breast imaging, as a branch of diagnostic radiology, entails a variety of imaging methods:

- Screening mammography uses a low-dose X-ray to identify breast cancer before symptoms appear. This enables early diagnosis and therapy. Every two years, women aged 50 to 74 in Australia are offered free breast screening.

- When symptoms are present, diagnostic mammography employs X-rays to make a diagnosis. The mammogram determines if the abnormalities are benign (non-cancerous) or whether breast cancer is present and treatment is required.

- Breast tomosynthesis is a revolutionary digital mammography technology that uses X-rays to create 3D images of the breast.

- Breast ultrasound is used to distinguish cysts (fluid-filled lumps) from solid lumps that may or may not be cancerous.

- Breast MRIs are used to detect early breast cancer in high-risk women and to establish the degree of any diagnosed breast cancer.

Breast core biopsy and fine needle aspiration (FNA) are two other breast imaging methods. As well as breast hookwire localization and vacuum-assisted core biopsy (Inside Radiology, 2016d).

Cardiac Imaging

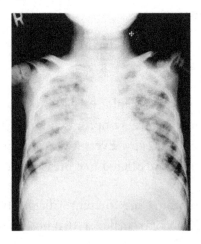

Cardiac imaging is a diagnostic radiology specialization. A cardiac radiologist directs or performs medical imaging to diagnose heart disorders such as heart disease, leaky heart valves, and problems in the size and structure of the heart (Inside Radiology, 2016e).

Imaging techniques used by a cardiac radiologist include X-rays, ultrasound (echocardiograms), CT scans, and MRI scans. Physicians use these tests to screen for heart disease, diagnose what is causing your symptoms, monitor your heart, and assess whether your therapy is effective. CT Coronary Angiography (CTCA), Coronary Artery Calcium Scoring, and MRI Heart (Cardiac MRI) are all cardiac (heart) imaging techniques (Inside Radiology, 2016e).

Musculoskeletal Imaging

Musculoskeletal imaging is a diagnostic radiology specialty that involves the ordering and interpretation of medical images of bones, joints, and corresponding soft tissues to diagnose injuries and disease. X-rays/plain radiography; fluoroscopy (a continuous X-ray that creates moving images of the functioning of joints and soft tissue); CT scans; ultrasound, which is used to image the anatomy and function of soft tissue around bones and joints; MRI scans; and imaging-guided pain management are all used by musculoskeletal imaging radiologists (Inside Radiology, 2016c).

Formative Assessment Questions:

1. How should you arrange the code sets when billing for E/M services?

2. Why would certain patients experience problems or complications with anesthesia?

3. In interventional radiology, why is the need for traditional or keyhole surgery eliminated?

4. H0w or which radiation methods are used to destroy cancerous cells?

5. What are some examples of abdominal imaging tests?

Key Concepts

- **Diagnostic radiology** is a medical specialty that entails performing a variety of imaging procedures in order to gather images of the inside of the body.

- Diagnostic imaging tests involve X-rays, CT (computed tomography) scans, MRI (magnetic resonance imaging) scans, ultrasound examinations (also known as sonography), and nuclear medicine imaging techniques.

- Diagnostic radiologists use these images **to determine illnesses** or **injuries.**

- **Interventional radiology** utilizes a range of imaging techniques, which include X-rays, MRIs, fluoroscopy, CT scans, and ultrasounds.

- Interventional radiologists treat tumors, perform organ biopsies, and place stents by inserting tiny instruments and catheters into the body through an artery or vein.

- **Radiation oncology** treats cancer and many non-malignant diseases with radiation. Types of high-energy radiation used are high-energy X-rays, electron beams, and gamma rays.

- Types of imaging include **abdominal imaging, breast imaging, cardiac imaging,** and **musculoskeletal imaging.**

CHAPTER 6:

LABORATORY AND PATHOLOGY

The Pathology and Laboratory part provides codes for the numerous medical tests specialists run to discover the origin of a patient's illness. Blood tests, drug tests, urinalysis, hematology, and other examinations may be performed (Medical Billing and Coding, 2021).

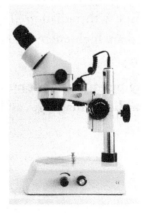

Some of the tests and the code ranges they occupy include:

Field	Range	Field	Range
Organ or Disease-oriented Panels	80047–80076	Drug Testing	80100–80104
Therapeutic Drug Assays	80150–80299	Evocative/Suppression Testing	80400–80440
Consultations (Clinical Pathology)	80500–80502	Urinalysis	81000–81099
Molecular Pathology	81200–81479	Multianalyte Assays with Algorithmic Analyses	81500–81599
Chemistry	82000–84999	Hematology and Coagulation	85002–85999
Immunology	86000–86849	Transfusion Medicine	86850–86999
Microbiology	87001–87999	Anatomic Pathology	88000–88099
Cytopathology	88104–88199	Cytogenic Studies	88230–88299
Surgical Pathology	88300–88399	In Vivo Laboratory Procedures	88720–99749
Other Procedures	89049–89240	Reproductive Medicine Procedures	89250–89398

(Medical Billing and Coding, 2021)

Path and Lab have two types of general tests: qualitative and quantitative. Quantitative tests determine how much of a material (such as calcium or alcohol) is present in the body, whereas qualitative testing determines the presence of a substance in general. The number of tests completed, rather than the results of the tests, is used to calculate Path and Lab codes. That is, if you tested for Phenobarbital and alcohol, you would record them as two procedures (Medical Billing and Coding, 2021).

Let's have a look at the first set of panels. Panels are a collection of biological samples, such as blood, that are evaluated in a lab. Each panel has specific criteria. A comprehensive metabolic panel, for instance, needs to check for albumin, carbon dioxide, potassium, sodium, total protein, as well as nine other chemicals. What the panels need depends on the system or pathology that the panel is attempting to determine. The next section is drug testing. The first portion of this chapter contains qualitative assays. They look for the presence of drugs. Then there are the drug assays. Each kind of drug has its own code. All of these drug assay codes are quantitative (e.g., how much lidocaine is in the system) (Medical Billing and Coding, 2021).

A number of pathological tests are also included in the Path and Lab section. Molecular pathology procedures examine genes, antigens, and a variety of other biological processes to determine the probability of a disorder or confirm a diagnosis. For example, a test for a genetic predisposition to a certain form of breast cancer can be found under this section (Medical Billing and Coding, 2021).

The chemistry section follows molecular pathology. This section contains tests for specific chemical substances that can provide information to a pathologist or physician regarding the patient's condition. The immunology chapter is similar. The tests in this area aid in determining the presence or response of various essential chemicals in the body that are associated with the immune system. Tests for specific allergies and quantitative assays for tumor antigens are included here (Medical Billing and Coding, 2021).

Microbiological tests are also covered in Path and Lab. These tests detect organisms such as giardia, rubeola, hepatitis, and HIV. Each microbiological organism has its own set of codes. Anatomic pathology, surgical pathology, and a variety of other methods of pathological investigation round out the section. Procedure codes for autopsies can be found in anatomic pathology (Medical Billing and Coding, 2021).

Human tissue is examined in surgical pathology. When tissue is removed for examination, a Path and Lab code is assigned. There is a Path and Lab code for a bone marrow biopsy performed by a surgeon. The same is true for an adrenal gland excision or a mastectomy. These surgical pathology codes are classified according to their level. Each level is quite large and covers a wide variety of topics. They are classified based on the difficulty and/or cost of the excision or resection operation. As a result, the more difficult or expensive it is to collect a tissue sample, the higher the level of surgical pathology code you will require (Medical Billing and Coding, 2021).

Path and Lab tests performed during surgery are also included in surgical pathology codes. The CPC exam will almost certainly include a question about this. During this procedure, a pathologist evaluates a tissue sample to ensure that the surgeon has removed the required amount of tissue (Medical Billing and Coding, 2021).

Formative Assessment Questions:

1. How does the medical anesthesiologist ensure that the patient is stable under general anesthesia?
2. How do interventional radiologists identify injury and disease using imaging techniques?
3. What is the difference between qualitative and quantitative tests in pathology and laboratory?
4. Why would a pathologist need to evaluate a tissue sample during surgery?

Key Concepts

- Path and lab have two types of general tests: qualitative and quantitative.

  - **Quantitative tests** determine how much of a material (such as calcium or alcohol) is present in the body.

  - **Qualitative testing** determines the presence of a substance in general.

- **Panels** are a collection of biological samples, such as blood, that are evaluated in a lab.

- **Drug testing** includes qualitative and drug assays.

- **Molecular pathology** procedures examine genes, antigens, and a variety of other biological processes to determine the probability of a disorder or confirm a diagnosis.

- The **chemistry section** contains tests for specific chemical substances that can provide information to a pathologist or physician regarding the patient's condition.

- The **immunology section** aids in determining the presence or response of various essential chemicals in the body that are associated with the immune system.

- **Microbiological tests** detect organisms such as giardia, rubeola, hepatitis, and HIV.

CHAPTER 7:

MEDICINE

Non-invasive or minimally invasive diagnostic and therapeutic procedures and services are classified in the CPT Medicine section. Non-invasive techniques do not necessitate any surgical incisions or excisions and are not open procedures. Percutaneous access is one of the minimally invasive methods. CPT's final section is medicine, and its codes can be reported alongside those from all other sections (Green, 2010).

The Medicine section categorizes procedures and services that are procedure-oriented (e.g., immunizations), that apply to various medical specialties (e.g., gastroenterology, ophthalmology, otorhinolaryngology, and psychiatry), and that apply to various types of healthcare providers (e.g., physical therapists and occupational therapists) (Green, 2010). Medicine subsections include the following:

7.1 Immune Globulins

Immune globulins (Ig) (gamma globulins or immune serum glob-ulins) are sterilized solutions derived from pooled human blood plasma that contain immunoglobulins (or antibodies) that pro-tect against infectious organisms that cause a variety of diseases. (Antibodies are components found in blood plasma that help the body fight infection.) Immune globulins are given to patients who need to use someone else's antibodies to fight off or avoid infections. High levels of antibodies against hepatitis B (Hepatitis B Immune Globulin-HBIG), rabies (Rabies Immune Globulin-RIG), teta-nus (Tetanus Immune Globulin-TIG), and varicella (chicken pox; Varicella Zoster Immune Globulin-VZIG) are found in Ig formula-tions produced from donors (Green, 2010).

Immune globulin codes (90281–90399) are used for the supply of the immune globulin product, which contains broad-spectrum and anti-infective immune globulins, antitoxins, and other isoantibod-ies. Immune globulin administration is reported individually using a code from the Medicine section's Therapeutic, Prophylactic, and Diagnostic Injections and Infusions subsection (Green, 2010).

7.2 Immunization Administration for Vaccines/Toxoids

Immunization administration for vaccines/toxoids codes (90465–90474) (and vaccines/toxoids subsection codes, 90476–90749) include the following:

- Administrative staff services (e.g., appointment scheduling, patient record preparation, and insurance claim submission to a payer)

- Clinical staff services (e.g., vital sign taking, analyzing previous responses and contraindications, preparing and administering the vaccine/toxoid, monitoring reactions, and documenting in the record)

The following kinds of immunization administration for vaccines/toxoids are reported:

- Subcutaneous, percutaneous, intramuscular, and intradermal injections

- Oral and intranasal administration (Green, 2010)

Pediatric vaccine/toxoid immunization administration is coded 90465–90468 to appropriately describe the work performed, which includes patient/family counseling offered by the physician during vaccine/toxoid administration. (Codes 90465–90468 are reported when the physician gives face-to-face counseling to the patient/family during vaccine/toxoid administration. When face-to-face therapy is not offered, report codes 90471–90474, according to the CPT) (Green, 2010).

7.3 Vaccines, Toxoids

Vaccines/toxoids codes (90476–90749) are exclusively used to identify the vaccine/toxoid product. They are reported in addition to vaccine/toxoids administration codes (90465–90474) (Green, 2010).

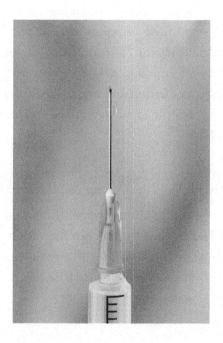

Reporting E/M Service Codes with Immunization Administration for Vaccines/ Toxoids and Vaccines, Toxoids Codes

There is much uncertainty about whether a provider should record an evaluation and management (E/M) service for an immunization administration of vaccines/toxoids encounter. The correct coding is determined by whether or not the provider administered a medically essential E/M service in addition to the immunization administration. To be assigned an E/M code in addition to the vaccination administration code, the E/M service must be more extensive than the services included with immunization administration codes. When a separate E/M service is provided (e.g., history, physical examination, and medical decision-making), a separate E/M code (99201–99215) is recorded in addition to the applicable code for immunization administration, and the code for the vaccine/toxoid product. Modifier -25 is added to the E/M code (significant, individually identifiable evaluation and management service provided by the same physician on the same day as the treatment or other service) (Green, 2010).

Link an appropriate ICD-9-CM code that defines the problem treated to the E/M code to clearly prove the medical necessity of the E/M service. The provider should additionally document a distinct note for the E/M service (different from the vaccination history and vaccine/toxoid note, which includes the product, lot number, site and method, and VIS date) (Green, 2010).

7.4 Psychiatry

Psychotherapy services are reported by psychiatrists, psychologists, and licensed clinical social workers using psychiatry codes (90801–90899), which include the following headings and subheadings:

- Procedures for psychiatric diagnostic or evaluation interviews

- Psychiatric therapeutic treatments

- Office or another type of outpatient facility

- Psychotherapy that is insight-focused, behavior-modifying, or supportive

- Psychotherapy that is interactive

- Residential care institution, inpatient hospital, or partial hospital

  - Psychotherapy that is insight-oriented, behavior-modifying, and/or supportive

  - Psychotherapy that is interactive

- Other types of psychotherapy

- Other psychiatric procedures or services (Green, 2010)

Psychiatric Diagnostic or Evaluative Interview Procedures

Psychiatric diagnostic or evaluation interview services (90801–90802) include the following:

- History and examination

- Assessment of mental state

- Patient disposition

- Communication with family members or other sources

- Order and medical interpretation of laboratory or other diagnostic studies (Green, 2010)

Children are typically given interactive psychiatric diagnostic interviews and examination services. They include the use of physical aids (e.g., dolls) and non-verbal communication (e.g., drawing together) to overcome barriers to clinician-patient therapeutic engagement.

A comprehensive mental state evaluation comprises the following components:

- Time, place, and human orientation

- Recent and distant memory

- Concentration and attention span

- Language (e.g., naming objects and repeating phrases)

- Knowledge bank (e.g., knowledge of current events, past history, and vocabulary)

- Mood and impact (e.g., depression, anxiety, agitation, or mania) (Green, 2010)

Psychiatric Therapeutic Procedures

The following are classified as psychiatric therapy services codes (90804–90899):

- Insight-oriented behavior-modifying, and/or supportive psychotherapy in an office or other outpatient facility, as well as interactive psychotherapy

- Insight-oriented, behavior-modifying and/or supportive, and interactive psychotherapy in an inpatient or partial hospital, or residential care facility

- Other types of psychotherapy

- Other psychiatric procedures or services (Green, 2010)

Psychotherapy, often known as talk therapy, counseling, or psychosocial therapy, is the treatment of mental and emotional illnesses in which patients speak with a mental health practitioner (such as a psychiatrist) or therapist about their condition(s) and related difficulties (such as a psychotherapist or a licensed clinical social worker).

- Insight-oriented psychotherapy, also known as psychodynamic psychotherapy, is a method of treating mental illnesses and behavioral disorders through resolving unconscious psychological conflicts.

- Behavior-modifying psychotherapy is a type of treatment that focuses on changing harmful or unwanted behaviors. It often includes a desensitization system (facing something that generates anxiety), reinforcement of positive behavior, and rewards. Biofeedback and relaxation training may also be included (Green, 2010).

The psychiatric therapeutic procedures code is determined using the following criteria:

- Type of psychotherapy (e.g., interactive vs. insight-oriented, behavior-modifying, and/or supportive)

- Service location (e.g., office vs. inpatient)

- Face-to-face interaction with the patient

- Whether or not psychotherapy was coordinated with evaluation and management services (Green, 2010)

Psychoanalysis (90845) seeks to understand a patient's motivations and conflicts in order to alter maladaptive behavior (e.g., an inability to cope with the challenges of everyday living). Daily reports of the psychoanalysis code are recorded. Do not mix up psychoanalysis codes and psychotherapy codes. The psychoanalysis code refers to the practice of psychoanalysis (e.g., the patient is being treated by a physician who is qualified to conduct analytic therapy, and psychoanalysis is being used as a treatment) (Green, 2010).

Family psychotherapy engages the patient's family in the treatment process, and the psychotherapeutic sessions focus on the dynamics within the family. Family psychotherapy can be performed with or without the patient. The codes 90846–90849 are selected depending on whether or not the patient is present and whether or not numerous family groupings are being treated (Green, 2010).

The following are additional psychiatric services or procedures:

- Pharmacologic management

- Narcosynthesis

- Electroconvulsive therapy

- Individualized psychophysiological therapy with biofeedback training

- Hypnotherapy

- Medical management with environmental intervention

- Psychiatric review of hospital records

- Psychiatric examination/procedure results interpretation or explanation

- Reporting about a patient's psychiatric health, history, treatment, or progress to other physicians, agencies, or third-party payers (Green, 2010)

The evaluation of a patient's medications for affect (such as a patient's reaction to medication), proper dosage (e.g., a therapeutic dose), and renewal of prescribed medications is referred to as pharmacologic management. A physician (such as a psychiatrist) provides pharmacologic management to a patient who is receiving psychotherapy from a non-physician colleague (e.g., a psychologist or a licensed clinical social worker) or when a patient's disorder is well managed by psychotropic medicines alone. In most cases, the patient does not receive any additional services from the physician during the visit. When a physician provides an evaluation and management (E/M) service, pharmacologic management is included. It is not separately coded and reported. (The psychotherapy administered during pharmacologic management is low and is not coded or reported separately) (Green, 2010).

Narcosynthesis is a type of psychotherapy that is administered to a patient while they are under the influence of a drug, such as a sedative or narcotic (e.g., a barbiturate or benzodiazepine-type medication supplied intravenously). The administration of a drug to relieve inhibitions helps a patient to discuss concerns that might otherwise be too difficult to express verbally (Green, 2010).

Electroconvulsive therapy, which involves applying an electric current to the brain via scalp electrodes, is used to treat depression or life-threatening psychosis (e.g., severe affective disorders or schizophrenia). A convulsive response to electrical stimuli is referred to as electroconvulsive. It is vital to monitor the patient during electro-convulsive therapy (e.g., seizure control, observation, and treatment decisions). Report the required anesthetic code (00104), which includes heart and oxygen saturation monitoring, if the psychiatrist also administers anesthesia for the electroconvulsive therapy (Green, 2010).

7.5 Biofeedback

Biofeedback is a therapy that teaches patients how to manage autonomic body functions.

The following biofeedback services are available:

- Examining the patient's history

- Setting up the biofeedback apparatus

- Applying electrodes to the patient

- Responses must be read and interpreted

- Patient observation

- Muscle response control

Code 90901 represents the provision of biofeedback in the absence of psychophysiological therapy. Although other types of administration (e.g., electromyogram application) may be included in biofeedback services, code 90901 is meant to identify all methods of biofeedback supplied, even when more than one modality is applied during the same session. An electromyogram is a type of nerve-conduction examination that records the electrical activity produced by muscle contractions. Manometry is a diagnostic procedure that uses a pressure-sensitive tube to detect muscular function (Green, 2010).

7.6 Dialysis

The following headings are included in the Dialysis subsection (90935–90999):

- Hemodialysis

- Various dialysis procedures

- Services for end-stage renal disease

- Other dialysis treatments (Green, 2010)

Renal dialysis eliminates harmful waste products from the body when the patient's kidneys are unable to do so due to disease or deterioration. Dialysis is used in the treatment of acute, temporary kidney failure (e.g., acute renal failure) or chronic renal failure (e.g., end-stage renal disease). Depending on the patient's health and whether the patient has acute or chronic renal failure, the following methods of dialysis are used:

- Hemodialysis is the process of eliminating waste materials, toxins, and excess fluids from the blood; the patient's blood is redirected into a dialyzer, where it is treated before being reintroduced to the patient's circulation via another tube inserted into a different blood vessel.

- Peritoneal dialysis involves inserting a soft catheter into the abdominal cavity and infusing dialysate fluid at regular intervals (Green, 2010).

Hemodialysis

All E/M services connected to the patient's renal condition on the day of the hemodialysis treatment are included in hemodialysis service codes 90935–90940. These codes are used to report hemodialysis services provided to end-stage renal disease (ESRD) and non-ESRD patients in an inpatient setting, as well as non-ESRD patients in an outpatient environment (Green, 2010).

Miscellaneous Dialysis Procedures

Codes 90945–90999 for miscellaneous dialysis procedures include the following:

- Hemofiltration, peritoneal dialysis, and other ongoing renal replacement therapy (90945–90947) (for single physician evaluation or repeated physician evaluations)

- Dialysis training (90989–90993) (e.g., a finished training course or an individual training session)

- Hemoperfusion (90997) (e.g., using activated charcoal or resin)

- Dialysis procedure not listed (inpatient or outpatient) (90999) (Green, 2010)

End-Stage Renal Disease (ESRD) Services

ESRD services (90951–90970) are often provided as outpatient procedures, with compensation based on a monthly capitated payment approach.

- ESRD service codes are recorded once per patient every month (every 30 days). The relevant code is only reported once, at the end of a month of ESRD services.

- When a patient receives less than a full month of services, ESRD service codes are reported. The relevant code is reported for each day of care (e.g., when a patient requires

ESRD services for less than a month following inpatient hospitalization) (Green, 2010).

7.7 Gastroenterology

The Gastroenterology subsection (91000–91299) consists of the following headings:

- Gastric physiology

- Other procedures

The Surgery section contains procedures for gastroenterology. Pathology, Laboratory, and Radiology sections include related diagnostic services (Green, 2010).

7.8 Ophthalmology

General Ophthalmological Services

Examinations for new or established patients are documented using the general ophthalmological services codes (92002–92142). Instead of a general ophthalmological service code, a physician (such as an ophthalmologist) can record an appropriate E/M service code. Reporting both an E/M service code and the general ophthalmological services code (92002–92014) is not recommended. Because they provide unique and specialized services that do not satisfy criteria connected with E/M codes, ophthalmologists have a decision when assigning codes for E/M services. An ophthalmologist may report codes from the Medicine section instead of the E/M section. CPT codes 92002–92014 describe intermediate and comprehensive levels of service. When the ophthalmologist provides services that are less than those identified by codes 92002–92014, the corresponding E/M codes should be reported (99201–99215) (Green, 2010).

- History, general medical observation, external ocular and adnexal examination, and additional diagnostic tests as necessary are all part of intermediate ophthalmological services. This could include using mydriasis for ophthalmoscopy.

- Comprehensive ophthalmological services encompass a comprehensive assessment of the entire visual system, including tonometry and biomicroscopy as well as history, general medical observation, external and ophthalmoscopic examinations, gross visual fields, and a basic sensorimotor examination. Diagnostic and therapy procedures are also provided. Comprehensive services may be provided over the course of many sessions or visits (Green, 2010).

Special Ophthalmological Services

Services that are not considered part of a general ophthalmological examination are coded as special ophthalmological services. They are regarded as significant, individually identifiable services, which implies that when performed, their codes are reported in addition to codes for general ophthalmological examination services. Determination of refractive state (92015) determines if vision correction requires a prescription. It is carried out with the aid of an eye chart and a refractor (a device that carries a variety of lens strengths that can be easily and quickly changed). The determination of refractive state services does not involve the fitting of glasses or contact lenses. Code 92025 is assigned to computerized corneal topography (also known as computer-assisted keratography or videokeratography), in which a digital camera is used to capture an image of the patient's cornea for computer analysis (Green, 2010).

Contact Lens and Spectacle Services (Including Prosthesis for Aphakia)

The provision of contact lenses or spectacles (glasses) is not covered when contact lens or spectacle services are offered. Report the relevant HCPCS level II code for the material supply (Green, 2010).

7.9 Special Otorhinolaryngology Services

The following subheadings are included under Special Otorhinolaryngologic Services (92502–92700):

- Tests of vestibular function without electrical recording

- Vestibular function examinations with recording (e.g., ENG)

- Audiologic function examinations

- Services for evaluation and treatment

- Special diagnostic procedures

- Other procedures (Green, 2010)

When otorhinolaryngologic services are provided as part of an E/M service, the component procedures (e.g., otoscopy, tuning fork test, whispered voice test) should not be coded and reported separately. Special otorhinolaryngologic services (92502–92700) are listed individually since they are not normally included in a thorough otorhinolaryngologic evaluation. Evaluation services and function tests are covered under codes 92502–92526 (e.g., evaluation and treatment of speech, language, or hearing problems, assessment of laryngeal and facial nerve function). Both ears are tested in audiologic function tests with medical diagnostic evaluation codes (92551–92597). Modifier -50 (Bilateral Procedure) should not be added to these codes. When only one ear is serviced, add modifier -52 (Reduced Services) to the appropriate code (Green, 2010).

When calibrated electronic equipment is utilized, audiometric test codes (92551–92597) are reported individually. Earphones are used for pure-tone audiometry (92552–92553). The patient reacts to various tone pitches (frequencies). Air and bone thresholds (92553) What is the code range for dialysis? are similar to pure-tone audiometry procedures but instead of earphones, a bone oscillator is used (Green, 2010).

7.10 Cardiovascular

Therapeutic Services and Procedures

After the diagnostic images are collected, therapeutic services performed during a heart catheterization are recorded in addition to the heart catheterization codes (e.g., balloon angioplasty). The following are examples of therapeutic procedures:

- Cardiopulmonary resuscitation (CPR) (92950)

- Pacing transcutaneously (92953)

- Cardioversion (92960–92961)

- Procedures for Circulatory Assist (92970–92971)

- Thrombolysis (92975)

- Stent implantation by transcatheter (92980)

- Percutaneous transluminal coronary balloon angioplasty (PTCA) (92982)

- Atherectomy (92995)

Report code 92950 when CPR is performed in the absence of further evaluation and management services. Because critical-care and prolonged management services are time-based, when code 92950 is recorded separately, the time required to perform CPR is not factored into the critical care or other time-based evaluation and management services (Green, 2010).

Cardiography

Cardiography, also known as electrocardiography, is a diagnostic process that uses a cardiograph to capture the electronic activity of the heart and generates a cardiogram (or electrocardiogram, ECG, or EKG). Cardiography codes 93000–93278 are used to report routine electrocardiograms and additional procedures (e.g., vector cardiograms, 24-hour monitoring, and patient demand recordings when ordered by the provider). Before reporting cardiography codes, make sure you identify the total, professional, and technical components (as well as the applicable modifiers). Critical-care evaluation and management services include routine monitoring of EKG rhythm and hemodynamics, including cardiac outputs. As a result, do not report EKG rhythm strip and cardiac output measurement review codes (93040–93042, 93561, 93562) separately with critical-care services (Green, 2010).

Cardiovascular Device Monitoring – Implantable and Wearable Device

Cardiovascular monitoring services (e.g., pacemaker programming) are coded 93279–93299 (Green, 2010).

Echocardiography

Echocardiography is a diagnostic approach that uses ultrasound to provide two-dimensional pictures of the heart and major arteries (aorta, vena cavae). The total technique is included in the echocardiography codes (93307–93350). Add modifier -26 to the code when only the professional component is performed (Green, 2010).

Cardiac Catheterization

Cardiac catheterization is a multi-component invasive diagnostic medical procedure. The operation begins when the physician inserts one or more catheters into the patient's peripheral arteries and/or veins. Cardiac catheterizations encompass three distinct services:

- Cardiac catheterization (93501–93529)

- During cardiac catheterization, injection procedures are performed (93539–93545)

- Injection procedure, imaging supervision, interpretation, and reporting (93555–93556)

During cardiac catheterization operations, cardiac output measurements (e.g., codes 93561–93562) are frequently conducted. As a result, codes 93561–93562 are not recorded alongside cardiac catheterization codes. Fluoroscopic guiding techniques are an integral part of invasive intravascular procedures and are not coded separately. However, codes for fluoroscopic guided procedure supervision and interpretation are recorded separately (Green, 2010).

Stent insertion, atherectomy, and balloon angioplasty are all examples of percutaneous coronary artery interventions. Report only the most complex intervention for a given coronary artery and its branches, regardless of the number of stent placements, atherectomies, or balloon angioplasties performed in that coronary artery and its branches. (Stent placement is regarded as more complex than atherectomy.) An atherectomy is a more complicated procedure than balloon angioplasty.) Modifier -59 should not be added to codes for percutaneous coronary artery stent implantation, atherectomy, or balloon angioplasty (Green, 2010).

These interventions are reported with the relevant modifier to identify which coronary artery was treated. The following are the modifiers:

- LC (left circumflex coronary artery)

- LD (left anterior descending coronary artery)

- RC (right coronary artery) (Green, 2010)

Review patient-record documentation when reporting codes for cardiac catheterization procedures to determine the following:

- Catheter placement

- Injection procedure

- Supervision and interpretation (Green, 2010)

The femoral artery is the most commonly used access point for cardiac catheterization (including left heart catheterization, aortography, coronary angiography, internal mammary artery injection, vein bypass graft injection, and other left heart and coronary artery treatments). The right femoral vein is most commonly used for right heart catheterization and pulmonary arteriography. The catheters are subsequently placed in a branch vessel or a heart chamber. During the catheterization procedure, measurements of intracardiac and intravascular pressure, oxygen saturation or blood gasses, and cardiac output are recorded (Green, 2010).

Angiography, which is routinely performed during a diagnostic catheterization, requires the use of a separate code. Angiography includes injecting a contrast medium into the vessel and imaging it. During the process, repositioning the catheter may be required to inject contrast for angiography. A final analysis of the data, as well as a report, are necessary. Endomyocardial biopsy (93505) obtains myocardial tissue samples for direct pathologic examination of cardiac muscle using a specialized biopsy catheter with a bioptome tip (an open tip that closes to retrieve tissue sample). A bioptome-tip catheter is inserted and advanced to the right ventricle under fluoroscopy to monitor a heart transplant patient for signs of rejection. The instrument extracts myocardial tissue that is sent for pathologic testing (Green, 2010).

The cardiac catheterization codes include the insertion of a Swan-Ganz catheter (93503). Swan-Ganz catheters are flexible, multiple-lumen, balloon-tipped flotation catheters that are inserted through a major peripheral vein (e.g., the jugular or subclavian). Under pressure waveform guidance, fluoroscopy is not required as it travels via the right atrium, right ventricle, and pulmonary arteries. After inflating the balloon, the tip monitors left ventricular end-diastolic pressure as well as central venous pressure. The catheter measures pulmonary artery systolic, diastolic, and mean pressures with the balloon deflated; it then enables infusion (and some patients are fitted with pacing electrodes) (Green, 2010).

Intracardiac Electrophysiological Procedures/Studies

Intracardiac electrophysiological operations and studies (93600–93662) describe services that record, map, or alter heart conduction (e.g., recording bundle of His, mapping tachycardia during repair surgery). Many of these codes include instructional notes indicating their compatibility with other codes. Intracardiac electrophysiological procedures (EP) can be diagnostic or therapeutic, and they involve catheter insertion and repositioning (Green, 2010).

Other Procedures

Cardiac rehabilitation is a tailored exercise and education routine. Cardiologists, nurse educators, dietitians, exercise rehabilitation experts, occupational therapists, physical therapists, psychologists, and psychiatrists collaborate with patients in cardiac rehabilitation programs that typically last three to six months. CPT codes 93797 and 93798 denote full cardiac rehabilitation services offered by a physician. This includes all cardiac rehabilitation-related services; therefore, reporting a separate E/M service code would be inappropriate unless it is an unrelated, individually identifiable service (Green, 2010).

7.11 Non-invasive Vascular Diagnostic Studies

Non-invasive vascular diagnostic studies (93875–93990) are categorized as follows:

- Cerebrovascular arterial studies

- Extremity arterial studies (including digits)

- Extremity venous studies (including digits)

- Visceral and penile vascular studies

- Extremity arterial-venous studies

Non-invasive vascular diagnostic studies (e.g., a duplex scan) use ultrasound to show two-dimensional structure and motion, and the codes identify arterial and venous studies. They also identify anatomic features or locations that need to be examined. (A duplex scan is a non-invasive test used to assess blood flow in a vessel) (Green, 2010).

7.12 Pulmonary

Therapeutic and diagnostic pulmonary services are coded 94002–94799. Report a code from 94002–94799 in addition to the relevant E/M code when pulmonary services are provided during an evaluation and management interaction (e.g., hospital inpatient visit, emergency department service, office visit).

Pulmonary services include:

- Ventilator management is provided to patients in hospital inpatient and observation care settings, nursing institutions, and those receiving home care.

- Other procedures include laboratory tests and test interpretation (e.g., spirometry, vital capacity, thoracic gas volume, etc.) (Green, 2010).

7.13 Allergy and Clinical Immunology

Allergy Testing

To determine the source of a patient's allergies, allergy sensitivity tests are done on the skin (cutaneous) and mucous membranes (e.g., pollen as a source). Skin tests for allergies include:

- **Percutaneous puncture, prick, or scratch test**: Tiny drops of purified allergen extracts are pierced or scratched into the skin's surface. The test is used to discover pollen, mold, pet dander, dust mites, foods, insect venom, and penicillin allergies.

- **Intradermal test (intracutaneous)**: Purified allergen extracts are injected into the skin of the patient's arm. When an allergy to penicillin or insect venom is suspected, the test is carried out.

- **Epicutaneous patch test**: An allergen is applied to a patch that is placed on the skin. The test is used to identify contact dermatitis-causing chemicals such as latex, medicines, perfumes, preservatives, hair dyes, metals, and resins (Green, 2010).

Allergen Immunotherapy

Allergen immunotherapy (also known as allergy shots, allergy vaccinations, desensitization shots, or hyposensitization shots) uses small doses of allergens (allergens to which a patient reacts) to enhance the patient's tolerance to allergens. Codes 95115–95117 describe allergenic extract administration but do not include allergenic extract supply. Codes 95120–95134 are reported for complete service, which includes the provision of allergenic extracts (Green, 2010).

Allergen immunotherapy is administered on a regular basis; patients often receive treatment once or twice a week for three to six months, followed by once a month for three to five years. Treatment is usually divided into two stages:

- The preparation phase, during which patients receive shots once or twice a week for three to six months.

- The maintenance phase, in which patients receive shots every two to four weeks for at least five months or longer (Green, 2010).

Code 95144 is assigned to the preparation and delivery of single-dose antigens for administration by another physician. When reporting this code, the number of single-dose vials made and given should be specified. The antigen, its preparation, and the concentration/volume required for injections are all described under the codes 95145–95170. These codes are reported for the supply of antigen for future administration. When reporting these codes, the number of doses prepared and supplied must be mentioned. Injection administration is not covered by these codes (Green, 2010).

7.14 Endocrinology

Continuous glucose (blood sugar) monitoring for up to 72 hours entails the subcutaneous insertion of a sensor that sends data to a monitor. Every day, the patient calibrates the monitor (Green, 2010).

7.15 Neurology and Neuromuscular Procedures

Neurology and neuromuscular codes (95805–96020) are used to classify non-surgical diagnostic and therapeutic services (Green, 2010).

Sleep Testing

Sleep studies and polysomnography (95805–95811) are two types of sleep testing that are used to continuously monitor and record numerous physiological parameters of sleep for six or more hours. Sleep testing is typically performed at a health care facility's sleep laboratory, which is overseen by a sleep technologist who explains and conducts the sleep tests. (Physicians order, review, and interpret sleep studies and polysomnographies.) Regular (non-hospital) beds, an adjoining bathroom, and a television are typical features of sleeping rooms (Green, 2010).

Sleep testing codes (95805–95811) involve physician evaluation and interpretation of data, as well as report production.

- Multiple sleep latency (95805) is the measurement of a patient's sleep latency (dormancy) and/or alertness following the sleep period during at least a six-hour period of sleep.

- Sleep studies (95806–95807) assess adult and pediatric patients' brainwaves, heart rate, and eye movements while they sleep. They are used to diagnose sleep problems, which include nighttime breathing, movement, and neurologic conditions.

- Electrodes are placed on the scalp, sides of the head, below the chin, on the chest, and legs of the patient. To monitor airflow, a sensor is put near the nose and mouth. To measure blood oxygen levels, a pulse oximetry clip is positioned on the patient's finger. Patients are also recorded when they are sleeping.

- Polysomnography (95808–95811) is a sleep study that covers sleep staging as well as additional sleep parameters (e.g., belts can be placed around the rib cage and abdomen to measure breathing movements). A 1–4 lead EEG, electro-oculogram (EOG), and submental electromyogram (EMG) are all used in sleep staging. Parameters that determine the polysomnography code to report include the following:

- Airflow

- Body positions

- Continuous blood pressure monitoring

- Electrocardiogram

- End-tidal gas analysis

- Extended EEG monitoring

- Extremity muscle activity

- Gas exchange by oximetry

- Gastroesophageal reflux

- Motor activity-movement

- Penile tumescence

- Snoring

- Transcutaneous monitoring

- Ventilation and respiratory effort (Green, 2010)

Routine Electroencephalography (EEG)

When relevant, EEG codes 95812–95822 include the following:

- hyperventilation (deep or rapid breathing)

- photic stimulation (reaction to light)

To assess various stages of activity and sleep, extended EEG codes (95812–95813) are reported. When an electrocortigram is conducted during surgery (95829) or the physician inserts sphenoida electrodes for EEG recording (95830), codes 95829–95830 are reported (Green, 2010).

Muscle and Range-of-Motion Testing

Muscle and range-of-motion testing codes (95831–95857) are reported for muscle testing, range-of-motion measurements and reports, and Tensilon testing for myasthenia gravis. Tensilon (or its generic, edrophonium chloride) is injected into a vein to stop the action of the enzyme that breaks down the neurotransmitter acetylcholinesterase. The patient is then examined for rapid strength improvement (e.g., use of eye muscles) (Green, 2010).

Electromyography

Electromyography (EMG) is a test that measures nerve function by identifying the electrical activity generated by muscles. Needle electromyography testing requires inserting needle electrodes into skeletal muscles and measuring electrical activity in those muscles with an oscilloscope (a device that displays electrical waveforms on a monitor) and a loudspeaker (Green, 2010).

What is the code range for intracardiac electrophysiological operations and studies?

Intraoperative Neurophysiology

When conducted during a surgical procedure, the intraoperative neurophysiology testing add-on code 95920 is reported. (The primary procedure code is reported as the first procedure listed.) For each hour of testing, code 95920 is recorded (Green, 2010).

Autonomic Function Tests

Autonomic function tests, which examine the functioning of the autonomic nervous system (e.g., heart or lungs), are coded 95921–95923 (Green, 2010).

Evoked Potentials and Reflex Tests

A short-latency somatosensory evoked potential research involves electrically stimulating nerves to assess their responsiveness to the body's external and internal components (e.g., the organs). (The relevant code is reported based on the testing site.) A central motor-evoked potential study examines the nervous system's pathway by using low voltage electrodes placed on the scalp and target sites.

A central nervous system (CNS) visual evoked potential (VEP) test involves activating the eye with the checkerboard or flash technique and monitoring the patient's response. Sensors are used to track orbicularis oculi (blink) tests (Green, 2010).

Special EEG Tests

When a separately identifiable service is performed, continuous electroencephalographic monitoring services codes are reported (Green, 2010).

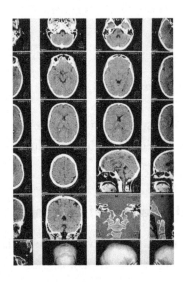

Neurostimulators, Analysis Programming

When a previously implanted neurostimulator pulse generator device is electrically evaluated to assess battery state, pulse amplitude and duration, rate, etc., codes 95970–95982 are reported (Green, 2010).

Other Procedures

The refill and maintenance of implantable infusion pumps or reservoirs are coded as 95990 and 95991. Per day, code 95992 is reported for Canalith repositioning. An unlisted neurological or neuromuscular diagnostic procedure is reported as code 95999 (Green, 2010).

Motion Analysis

Services performed during crucial diagnostic or therapeutic decision-making are coded 96000–96004. Patient movements are captured, digitized, copied to a computer, and processed during human motion analysis (Green, 2010).

Functional Brain Mapping

Code 96020 is assigned to functional brain mapping, which is a process in which a physician or a psychologist administers a series of tests to examine cognition, language, memory, movement, and sensation. The findings of the testing are recorded in a report to distinguish between expected and observed regions of brain activity when the patient performs given tasks (Green, 2010).

The patient is subjected to functional neuroimaging of the brain, also known as functional magnetic resonance imaging (fMRI) of the brain, during functional brain mapping. When a physician or psychologist fully delivers the functional brain mapping, report code 70555-51 in addition to code 96020 (Green, 2010).

7.16 Medical Genetics and Genetic Counseling Services

When a certified genetic counselor meets with an individual, couple, or family to study the family's genetic history and estimate risks connected with genetic disorders in offspring, code 96040 is reported (Green, 2010).

7.17 Central Nervous System (CNS) Assessments/Tests (Neuro-Cognitive, Mental Status, Speech Testing)

When tests are performed to measure the cognitive function of the central nervous system (e.g., cognitive processes, visual motor responses, and abstractive abilities), central nervous system assessments/tests codes (96101–96125) are reported. Psychological testing (code 96101), which comprises psychodiagnostic assessment of personality, psychopathology, emotionality, and intellectual ability, is one of the methods listed (e.g., WAI5-R, Rorschach, and MMPI tests). (Code 96101 is recorded for each hour in which the provider performed testing, analyzed test results, and generated the report) (Green, 2010).

7.18 Health and Behavior Assessment/Intervention

Health and behavior assessment/intervention codes (96150–96155) are assigned to tests that identify psychological, behavioral, emotional, cognitive, and social factors in the prevention, treatment, or management of physical health problems. The examination focuses on biopsychosocial aspects that are crucial to physical health problems and therapies rather than mental health. Procedures for health and behavior intervention are used to change problems that impact the patient. The intervention's goal is to improve the patient's health and well-being by the use of cognitive, behavioral, social, and/or psychophysiological procedures (Green, 2010).

Codes 96150–96155 identify services related to an acute or chronic illness that does not fulfill the requirements for psychiatric diagnosis, physical disability prevention, and health maintenance. Report the primary service performed if the patient requires psychiatric treatment (90801–90899) and/or health and behavior assessment/intervention (96150–96155). On the same date of service, do not record codes 96150–96155 in addition to codes 90801–90899 (Green, 2010).

7.19 Hydration, Therapeutic, Prophylactic, Diagnostic Injections and Infusions, and Chemotherapy and Other Highly Complex Drug or Highly Complex Biologic Agent Administration (96360–96549)

Codes 96360–96549 encompass the following services, which are not separately coded and reported:

- Local anesthesia administration

- Intravenous (IV) catheter insertion

- Access to an intravenous line, subcutaneous catheter, or port

- Syringes, tubing, and other common supplies

- Flushing is done after the infusion is completed

Report the initial code only once when numerous injections, or infusions, or combination services are delivered, unless two independent intravenous (IV) sites are necessary. Report the code based on actual infusion time when the length of infusion time is mentioned in the code description (Green, 2010).

Hydration

Hydration codes (96360–96549) are assigned to prepared fluids and electrolytes administered intravenously (e.g., normal saline and normal saline with potassium chloride). Examine the patient record for documentation that the physician supervised while reporting these codes:

- Patient evaluation (e.g., history and examination).

- Patient permission (e.g., discussion of risks and benefits).

- Patient safety (e.g., correct dose was given; patient response to infusion, including any adverse reactions).

- Staff that supplied infusion services (e.g., the nursing staff) (Green, 2010).

Therapeutic, Prophylactic, and Diagnostic Injections and Infusions

For the administration of substances (other than hydration), therapeutic, prophylactic, and diagnostic injections and infusions codes (96365–96379) are reported. Examine the patient record for documentation that the physician supervised while reporting these codes:

- Evaluation of the patient

- Consent of the patient

- Patient security

- Staff who performed injection and/or infusion services (Green, 2010)

Staff personnel who administer therapeutic, prophylactic, and diagnostic injections and infusions have extensive training in order to assess patients, offer informed consent, monitor patient safety, and administer injections and infusions. Codes 96374–96375 are reported for intravenous push, which is an injection given by a healthcare professional who is there at all times to administer the injection and examine the patient; lasting 15-minutes or less infusion (Green, 2010).

7.20 Chemotherapy and Other Highly Complex Drug or Highly Complex Biologic Agent Administration

Chemotherapy is the use of medications to eliminate cancer cells or restrict their growth, prevent cancer from spreading to other parts of the body, and prevent the recurrence of the cancer. Adjuvant chemotherapy refers to chemotherapy that is given in addition to other cancer treatments such as surgery and/or radiation therapy. Codes 96401–96549 denote parenteral administration of chemotherapeutic medicines, which means that the chemotherapy is administered through a method other than oral administration, such as implantation (of a catheter or port), infusion, or injection (Green, 2010).

There are numerous chemotherapy medications available to treat cancer today, and chemotherapy is delivered in a variety of methods based on the drugs used and the type of cancer. Oral chemotherapy is administered orally in the form of a pill, capsule, or liquid, whereas parenteral chemotherapy delivery methods include the following:

- The insertion of a catheter or a port into a central vein or bodily cavity

- Intravenous (IV) chemotherapy infusion or injection into a vein

- Intramuscular chemotherapy (IM) is injected into the muscle

- Subcutaneous (SQ) chemotherapy is injected beneath the skin (Green, 2010)

The parenteral modalities of chemotherapy administration are identified by the codes 96401–96549. When several methods of parenteral chemotherapy administration (e.g., injection, infusion, implantation) are utilized during the same encounter, providing a separate code for each parenteral method. When an intravenous infusion of saline (an antiemetic) or another non-chemotherapy medicine is given simultaneously with the chemotherapeutic agent(s), it is not coded and reported separately. The supply of the medications, on the other hand, is documented separately using HCPCS Level II codes. If the hydration or intravenous infusion is given on the same day, but sequentially rather than simultaneously with the chemothera-peutic drugs, the infusions are coded 96360–96368 (Green, 2010).

The parenteral modalities of chemotherapy administration are iden-tified by the codes 96401–96549. When various methods of paren-teral chemotherapy administration (e.g., injection, infusion, implan-tation) are used during the same encounter, provide a separate code for each parenteral method. When an intravenous infusion of saline (an antiemetic) or another non-chemotherapy medicine is given simultaneously with the chemotherapeutic agent(s), it is not coded and reported separately. The supply of the medications, on the other hand, is documented separately using HCPCS Level II codes. If the hydration or intravenous infusion is given on the same day, but sequentially rather than simultaneously with the chemotherapeutic drugs, the infusions are coded 96360–96368 (Green, 2010).

7.21 Photodynamic Therapy

Photodynamic therapy administered by external application of light to destroy malignancies or endoscopic application of light that activates photosensitive drugs to destroy abnormal tissue is coded 96567–96571 (Green, 2010).

The application of a photosensitizing agent (e.g., 20% topical ami-nolevulinic acid HCl) directly onto a patient's lesions to treat prema-lignant cells (e.g., non-hyperkeratotic actinic keratosis) or malignant cells is known as photodynamic therapy (PDT). The patient returns for a scheduled appointment during which the treated lesions are directed with a photodynamic therapy illuminator (light). When the topical agent applied to the lesions is irradiated, a cytotoxic reaction occurs, killing premalignant or malignant cells and preventing their spread (Green, 2010).

7.22 Special Dermatological Procedures

Special dermatological procedure codes (96900–96999) describe dermatological procedures that are typically (but not always) performed in conjunction with an appropriate E/M service code (Green, 2010).

EXAMPLE: The dermatologist performed a detailed history and examination during a level 3 outpatient consultation encounter; medical decision-making was of low complexity. The dermatologist treated the two areas of acne frontalis with ultraviolet light (actinotherapy). 99243 and 96900-51 codes are reported (Green, 2010).

The rest of the Medicine section includes:

- Physical medicine and rehabilitation

- Medical nutrition therapy

- Acupuncture

- Osteo manipulative treatment

- Chiropractic manipulative treatment

- Education and training for patient self-management

- Non-face-to-face non-physician services

- Special services, procedures, and reports

- Qualifying circumstances for anesthesia

- Moderate (conscious) sedation

- Other services and procedures

- Home health procedures/services

- Medication therapy management services

Formative Assessment Questions:

1. How is breast tomosynthesis used?

2. How is molecular pathology used? And which code range would you use to identify tests in this section?

3. What is the difference between administrative and clinical staff services?

4. How is the correct coding determined when administering a vaccine?

5. Why are non-verbal communication and physical aids included in interactive psychiatric diagnostic interview services?

Key Concepts

- **Immune globulins** are sterilized solutions derived from pooled human blood plasma that contain immunoglobulins that protect against infectious organisms that cause a variety of diseases.

- Immune globulin codes **(90281–90399)** are used for the supply of the immune globulin product, which contains broad-spectrum and anti-infective immune globulins, antitoxins, and other isoantibodies.

- Immunization administration for **vaccines/toxoids codes (90465–90474)** includes the administrative and clinical staff services.

- Vaccines/toxoids codes **(90476–90749)** are exclusively used to identify the vaccine/toxoid product.

- **Psychotherapy services** are reported by psychiatrists, psychologists, and licensed clinical social workers using psychiatry codes (90801–90899).

- **Insight-oriented psychotherapy** is a method of treating mental illnesses and behavioral disorders through resolving unconscious psychological conflicts.

- **Behavior-modifying psychotherapy** is a type of treatment that focuses on changing harmful or unwanted behaviors.

- **Psychoanalysis** seeks to understand a patient's motivations and conflicts in order to alter maladaptive behavior.

- **Family psychotherapy** engages the patient's family in the treatment process, and the psychotherapeutic sessions focus on the dynamics within the family.

- **Narcosynthesis** is a type of psychotherapy administered to a patient while under the influence of a drug, such as a sedative or narcotic.

- **Electroconvulsive therapy**, which involves applying an electric current to the brain via scalp electrodes, is used to treat depression or life-threatening psychosis.

- **Biofeedback** is a therapy that teaches patients how to manage autonomic body functions.

- **Renal dialysis** eliminates harmful waste products from the body when the patient's kidneys are unable to do so due to disease or deterioration.

- All E/M services connected to the patient's renal condition on the day of the hemodialysis treatment are included in hemodialysis service codes **90935–90940**.

- Codes **90945–90999** for miscellaneous dialysis procedures include hemofiltration, peritoneal dialysis, and other ongoing renal replacement therapy; dialysis training; hemoperfusion; and dialysis procedures.

- **End-stage renal disease services (90951–90970)** are often provided as outpatient procedures.

- The **gastroenterology subsection (91000–91299)** comprises gastric physiology and other procedures.

- **General ophthalmological services** are coded **92002–92142**.

- **Special otorhinolaryngologic services** are coded **92502–92700**.

- Cardiovascular therapeutic procedures include cardiopulmonary resuscitation, pacing transcutaneously, cardioversion, circulatory assist procedures, thrombolysis, stent implantation by transcatheter, percutaneous transluminal coronary balloon angioplasty, and atherectomy.

- **Cardiography** is a diagnostic process that uses a cardiograph to capture the electronic activity of the heart and generates a cardiogram.

- **Cardiography codes 93000–93278** are used to report routine electrocardiograms and additional procedures.

- **Cardiovascular monitoring services** (e.g., pacemaker programming) are coded **93279–93299.**

- **Echocardiography** is a diagnostic approach that uses ultrasound to provide two-dimensional pictures of the heart and major arteries and is coded **93307–93350.**

- **Cardiac catheterization** is a multi-component invasive diagnostic medical procedure.

- **Intracardiac electrophysiological operations and studies (93600–93662)** describe services that record, map, or alter heart conduction.

- **Non-invasive vascular diagnostic studies (93875–93990)** include cerebrovascular arterial studies, extremity arterial studies, extremity venous studies, visceral and penile vascular studies, and extremity arterial-venous studies.

- **Therapeutic and diagnostic pulmonary services** are coded **94002–94799.**

- Skin tests for allergies include **percutaneous puncture, prick, or scratch test; intradermal test;** and **epicutaneous patch test.**

- **Allergen immunotherapy** uses small doses of allergens to enhance the patient's tolerance to allergens.

- **Neurology and neuromuscular codes (95805–96020)** are used to classify non-surgical diagnostic and therapeutic services.

- **Sleep studies and polysomnography (95805–95811)** are two types of sleep testing that are used to continuously monitor and record numerous physiological parameters of sleep for six or more hours.

- **Polysomnography (95808–95811)** is a sleep study covering sleep staging and additional sleep parameters.

- **Muscle and range-of-motion testing codes (95831–95857)** are reported for muscle testing, range-of-motion measurements and reports, and Tensilon testing for myasthenia gravis.

- **Electromyography** is a test that measures nerve function by identifying the electrical activity generated by muscles.

- **Autonomic function tests,** which examine the functioning of the autonomic nervous system, are coded 95921–95923.

- When a **previously implanted neurostimulator pulse generator device is electrically evaluated** to assess battery state, pulse amplitude and duration, rate, etc., **codes 95970–95982** are reported.

- The **refill and maintenance of implantable infusion pumps or reservoirs** are coded as **95990** and **95991**.

- Services performed during **crucial diagnostic or therapeutic decision-making** are coded **96000–96004.**

- When tests are performed to measure the cognitive function of the **central nervous system, central nervous system assessments/tests codes (96101–96125)** are reported.

- **Health and behavior assessment/intervention codes (96150–96155)** are assigned to tests that identify psychological, behavioral, emotional, cognitive, and social factors in preventing, treating, or managing physical health problems.

- Codes **96360–96549** encompass the following services: **local anesthesia administration; intravenous (IV) catheter insertion; access to an intravenous line, subcutaneous catheter, or port; syringes, tubing, and other common supplies; flushing.**

- **Hydration codes (96360–96549)** are assigned to prepared fluids and electrolytes administered intravenously.

- For the administration of substances (other than hydration), therapeutic, prophylactic, and diagnostic injections and infusions codes **(96365–96379)** are reported.

- **Chemotherapy** is the use of medications to eliminate cancer cells or restrict their growth, prevent cancer from spreading to other parts of the body, and prevent the recurrence of the cancer. Codes 96401–96549 denote parenteral administration of chemotherapeutic medicines.

- **Photodynamic therapy** administered by external application of light to destroy malignancies or endoscopic application of light that activates photosensitive drugs to destroy abnormal tissue is coded **96567–96571.**

- **Special dermatological procedure codes (96900–96999)** describe dermatological procedures that are typically performed in conjunction with an appropriate E/M service code.

CHAPTER 8:

INTERNATIONAL CLASSIFICATION OF DISEASES (ICD) LEVEL II

The ICD has a wide range of uses around the world and provides crucial knowledge on the range, causes, and effects of human disease and death. Clinical terminology coded with ICD serves as the basic foundation for disease recording and statistics in all stages of care, as well as cause-of-death certificates. These data and statistics aid payment systems, service planning, quality and safety, administration, and health services research. Diagnostic guidance connected to ICD categories standardizes data collection and allows for large-scale research (World Health Organization, 2022).

For all general epidemiological and health-management reasons, the ICD has essentially developed into a recognized international standard diagnostic classification. These include analyzing the overall health of population groups and tracking the incidence and prevalence of diseases and other health issues in connection to other variables, such as the characteristics and circumstances of the individuals affected. The ICD is not designed or appropriate for indexing distinct clinical entities. There are certain limitations to using the ICD for financial analyses, such as billing or resource allocation (World Health Organization, 2016).

The ICD can be used to categorize diseases and other health issues that are reported on many types of health and vital records. Its original purpose was to categorize causes of death as they were recorded at the time of death registration. Later, its scope was expanded to cover morbidity diagnoses. Although the ICD is primarily intended for the classification of diseases and injuries with a formal diagnosis, not every problem or cause for contacting health services can be classified in this manner. As a result, the ICD includes a wide range of signs, symptoms, aberrant findings, complaints, and social conditions that might be used in place of a diagnosis on medical records (World Health Organization, 2016).

Therefore, it can be used to categorize data recorded under headings like "diagnosis," "reason for admission," "conditions treated," and "reason for consultation," which exist on a wide range of health records from which statistics and other health-situation information are derived (World Health Organization, 2016).

8.1 The Basic Structure and Principles of Classification of the ICD

The ICD is a categorization with variable axes. The structure evolved from that proposed by William Farr in the early days of international classification structure debates. His plan was for statistical data on diseases to be organized in the following way for all practical and epidemiological purposes:

- epidemic diseases

- constitutional or general diseases

- local diseases arranged by site

- developmental diseases

- injuries (World Health Organization, 2016)

This pattern can be found in the ICD-10 chapters. It has withstood the test of time and, while arbitrary in some aspects, is nevertheless considered to be a more useful structure for general epidemiological purposes than any of the alternatives studied. The first two and last two of the above-mentioned groups are 'special groups' that bring together conditions that would be inconveniently ordered for epidemiological investigation if they were scattered, such as in a categorization arranged primarily by anatomical site. The remaining group, 'local diseases arranged by site,' covers ICD chapters for each of the major body systems (World Health Organization, 2016).

The distinction between the chapters titled "special groups" and "body systems" has practical implications for understanding the structure of the classification, coding to it, and interpreting statistics based on it. It should be noted that conditions are generally grouped into one of the 'special groups' chapters. If there is any ambiguity about where a condition should be placed, the 'special groups' chapters should take precedence. The fundamental ICD is a single coded list of three-character categories, each of which can be subdivided into up to 10 four-character subcategories. In place of the previous versions' strictly numeric coding method, the tenth revision employs an alphanumeric code with a letter in the first position and a number in the second, third, and fourth positions. The fourth character comes after a decimal point. As a result, possible code numbers vary from A00.0 to Z99.9. The letter U is absent (World Health Organization, 2016).

8.2 Basic Coding Guidelines

Many terms not found in Volume 1 are found in the Alphabetical index, and coding requires that both the Alphabetical index and the Tabular list be reviewed before assigning a code.

Before proceeding to code, the coder must understand the concepts of classification and coding and have completed practical exercises.

The following is a brief guide designed to help the occasional user of the ICD:

1. Determine the type of statement to be coded and go to the Alphabetical index section. (If the statement refers to an illness, injury, or other condition covered in Chapters I–XIX or XXI–XXII of the index, reference Section I. Consult Section II if the statement is the external cause of an injury or other incident that falls under the scope of Chapter XX Section II.)

2. Find the lead term. This is usually a noun for the pathological condition in the case of diseases and injuries. However, some conditions represented as adjectives or eponyms are included as lead terms in the Alphabetical index.

3. Any note that appears under the lead word should be read and followed.

4. Read any terms contained in parentheses following the lead term (these modifiers have no effect on the code number), as well as any terms indented after the lead term (these modifiers may have an effect on the code number), until all of the words in the diagnostic expression have been reviewed.

5. Follow any cross-references ('see' and 'see also') found in the Alphabetical index with caution.

> What is the function of lymph nodes?

6. Check the Tabular list to ensure that the code number you've chosen is appropriate. A three-character code in the Alphabetical index with a dash in the fourth position indicates the presence of a fourth character in Volume 1. Further subdivisions for supplemental character positions are not indexed and must be found in Volume 1.

7. Any inclusion or exclusion terms under the specified code, or under the chapter, block, or category name, should be followed.

8. Assign the code (World Health Organization, 2016).

Formative Assessment Questions:

1. What are some of the pathology and laboratory tests specialists run to discover the origins of a patient's illness?

2. How is the provision of biofeedback in the absence of psychophysiological therapy coded?

3. Under which circumstances is dialysis used?

4. How has the ICD evolved from its original purpose?

5. How should statistical data be organized according to William Farr?

6. What should be reviewed before assigning an ICD-10 code?

Key Concepts

- Clinical terminology coded with ICD serves as the basic foundation for disease recording and statistics in all stages of care as well as cause-of-death certificates.

- The ICD has essentially developed into a recognized international standard diagnostic classification for all general epidemiological and health-management reasons.

- The ICD can be used to categorize diseases and other health issues that are reported on many types of health and vital records.

- ICD is organized as such per the proposal of William Farr:

  - Epidemic diseases

  - Constitutional or general diseases

  - Local diseases arranged by site

  - Developmental diseases

  - Injuries

CHAPTER 9:

ICD-10-CM CODING GUIDELINES

9.1 Certain Infectious and Parasitic Diseases: A00–B99

The ICD-10 code range (A00–B99); ICD-10 codes for Intestinal infectious diseases are included in this range. These include: tuberculosis, zoonotic bacterial infections, and other bacterial infections, diseases that are primarily transmitted sexually, other spirochetal disorders, other diseases induced by chlamydia, rickettsioses, infections of the central nervous system caused by viruses and prion proteins, viral hemorrhagic fevers and arthropod-borne viral fevers, infections caused by viruses that cause skin and mucous membrane lesions, other herpesviruses in humans, hepatitis virus, human immunodeficiency virus (HIV) infection, other viral diseases, protozoal diseases, mycoses, helminthiases, pediculosis, acariasis, and other parasitic infections sequelae of parasitic and infectious diseases, infectious bacterial and viral agents, other infectious diseases (American Association of Professional Coders, 2022b).

9.2 Neoplasms: C00–D49

ICD-10 Code Range (C00–D49), Neoplasms comprises ICD-10 codes for malignant neoplasms, in situ neoplasms, and benign neoplasms, excluding benign neuroendocrine tumors. Neoplasms of indeterminate behavior, polycythemia vera and myelodysplastic syndromes, benign neuroendocrine tumors, and neoplasms of unspecified behavior (American Association of Professional Coders, 2022t).

9.3 Diseases of the Blood and Blood-Forming Organs and Certain Disorders Involving the Immune Mechanism: D50–D89

ICD-10 codes for various forms of anemia are found in diseases of the blood and blood-forming organs, as well as certain immune-related conditions. In addition to bone marrow failure syndrome and coagulation defects, purpura and other hemorrhagic disorders are found in this range. This section includes abnormalities of the blood and blood-forming organs, as well as intraoperative and postoperative spleen complications, and certain immune-related disorders (American Association of Professional Coders, 2022e).

9.4 Endocrine, Nutritional and Metabolic Diseases: E00–E89

Endocrine, nutritional, and metabolic diseases cover ICD-10 codes for thyroid gland problems and diabetes mellitus. These are in addition to various disorders of glucose regulation and pancreatic internal secretion, and other endocrine gland illnesses. This code range covers intraoperative endocrine system complications, malnutrition, and other nutritional deficits, as well as overweight, obesity, and other forms of hyperalimentation; metabolic disorders; and unclassified postprocedural endocrine and metabolic problems and disorders (American Association of Professional Coders, 2022o).

9.5 Mental, Behavioral, and Neurodevelopmental Disorders: F01–F99

ICD-10 codes covering mental disorders caused by established physiological abnormalities, as well as mental and behavioral disorders caused by psychoactive substance use, are included in the category of mental, behavioral, and neurodevelopmental disorders. Furthermore, F20–F29 code schizophrenia, schizotypal, delusional, and other non-mood psychotic disorders. This range also includes mood [affective] disorders, anxiety, dissociative, stress-related, somatoform, and other non-psychotic mental disorders. In addition, behavioral syndromes, adult personality problems, and intellectual deficits are also coded within this range. Pervasive and particular developmental disorders, behavioral and emotional disorders which start often in childhood and adolescence, and unspecified mental disorder codes are F80–F99 (American Association of Professional Coders, 2022s).

9.6 Diseases of the Nervous System: G00–G99

ICD codes for inflammatory diseases of the central nervous system are included under Diseases of the Nervous System. They also comprise systemic atrophies that largely affect the central nervous system, extrapyramidal and movement disorders, and other nervous system degenerative diseases. This range also includes demyelinating diseases of the central nervous system; episodic and paroxysmal disorders, and nerve, nerve root, and plexus anomalies. Within G60–G99, you can locate codes for polyneuropathies and other peripheral nervous system disorders; diseases of the myoneural junction and muscle, cerebral palsy and other paralytic syndromes, and other nervous system disorders (American Association of Professional Coders, 2022l).

9.7 Diseases of the Eye and Adnexa: H00–H59

Diseases of the eye and adnexa include ICD-10 codes for eyelid, lacrimal system, and orbit abnormalities. They also encompass conjunctival, scleral, corneal, iris, ciliary body, lens, choroid, and retinal abnormalities, as well as glaucoma. This range also includes disorders of the vitreous body and globe, optic nerve and visual pathways, ocular muscles, binocular movement, accommodation, and refraction codes. H53–H59.89 includes visual disturbances and blindness, other eye and adnexa disorders, and intraoperative and postprocedural problems, and eye and adnexa disorders not otherwise classified (American Association of Professional Coders, 2022i).

9.8 Diseases of the Ear and Mastoid Process: H60–H95

Diseases of the ear and mastoid process include ICD codes for external ear, middle ear and mastoid, inner ear, and other ear disorders. H95–H95.89 are the codes classifying intraoperative and postprocedural complications, as well as ear and mastoid process disorders that are not otherwise classified (American Association of Professional Coders, 2022h).

9.9 Diseases of the Circulatory System: I00–I99

ICD-10 codes for acute rheumatic fever and chronic rheumatic heart disorders are included in Diseases of the Circulatory System. Hypertensive diseases, ischemic heart disease, pulmonary heart disease, and pulmonary circulation diseases are also included. This range also contains other types of heart disease, cerebrovascular diseases, and diseases of the arteries, arterioles, and capillaries. I80–I99 encompasses disorders of veins, lymphatic vessels, and lymph nodes that are not classified elsewhere, as well as other, unspecified circulatory system disorders (American Association of Professional Coders, 2022f).

9.10 Diseases of the Respiratory System: J00–J99

Respiratory diseases include ICD codes for acute upper respiratory infections, influenza, and pneumonia. Other acute lower respiratory infections, upper respiratory tract infections, and chronic lower respiratory diseases are also included. This code range also includes lung disorders induced by external agents, various respiratory diseases predominantly affecting the interstitium, and lower respiratory tract suppurative and necrotic conditions. J90–J99 encompasses various pleuritic diseases, intraoperative and postprocedural complications, and respiratory system disorders not elsewhere classified, as well as other respiratory system diseases (American Association of Professional Coders, 2022m).

9.11 Diseases of the Digestive System: K00–K95

ICD-10 codes for abnormalities of the oral cavity and salivary glands, esophagus, stomach, and duodenum, and the appendix are included in Diseases of the Digestive System. Hernias, non-infectious enteritis and colitis, other intestine diseases, and peritoneum and retroperitoneum diseases are also included. This range also includes diseases of the liver, gallbladder, biliary tract, pancreas, and other digestive system diseases (American Association of Professional Coders, 2022g).

9.12 Diseases of the Skin and Subcutaneous Tissue: L00–L99

Skin and subcutaneous tissue diseases include ICD codes for infections of the skin and subcutaneous tissue. Bullous disorders, dermatitis and eczema, papulosquamous disorders, and urticaria and erythema are also included. This range also includes radiation-related skin and subcutaneous tissue disorders, skin appendage disorders, and intraoperative and postprocedural problems of the skin and subcutaneous tissue. Other skin and subcutaneous tissue problems are covered by L80–L90 (American Association of Professional Coders, 2022n).

9.13 Diseases of the Musculoskeletal System and Connective Tissue: M00–M99

ICD-10 codes for arthropathies, dentofacial abnormalities [including malocclusion], and other jaw disorders are included in this range.

Systemic connective tissue disorders, dorsopathies, and soft tissue disorders are also included. M80–M96.89 include osteopathies and chondropathies, other musculoskeletal system and connective tissue disorders, and intraoperative and postprocedural complications and musculoskeletal system disorders not otherwise classified. This code range also includes periprosthetic fractures around the internal prosthetic joint and unclassified biochemical lesions (American Association of Professional Coders, 2022k).

9.14 Diseases of the Genitourinary System: N00–N99

Diseases of the Genitourinary System include ICD codes for kidney diseases such as chronic kidney disease, acute kidney failure, and renal tubulo-interstitial diseases. Urolithiasis, other kidney and ureter abnormalities, other urinary system diseases, and diseases of the male genital organs are also included. This range also encompasses breast problems, inflammatory diseases of female pelvic organs, non-inflammatory diseases of the female genital tract, and unclassified intraoperative and postprocedural complications and genitourinary system disorders (American Association of Professional Coders, 2022j).

9.15 Pregnancy, Childbirth, and the Puerperium: O00–O9A

Pregnancy, childbirth, and the puerperium includes ICD-10 codes for abortive pregnancy and high-risk pregnancy supervision. It also encompasses edema, proteinuria, and hypertensive disorders throughout pregnancy, childbirth, and puerperium; other maternal disorders primarily related to pregnancy; and maternal care relating to the fetus and amniotic cavity, as well as potential delivery complications. O60–09A include problems of labor and birth, delivery encounters, complications mostly connected to the puerperium, and other obstetric conditions not elsewhere classified (American Association of Professional Coders, 2022u).

9.16 Certain Conditions Originating in the Perinatal Period: P00–P96

Certain perinatal conditions include ICD codes for newborns impacted by maternal factors and complications of pregnancy, labor, and delivery. They also encompass newborn disorders related to gestational duration and fetal growth, abnormal findings on neonatal screening, and birth trauma. This code range also includes respiratory and cardiovascular disorders associated with the perinatal period, infections associated with the perinatal period, and neonatal hemorrhagic and hematological abnormalities. P70–P96 include transitory endocrine and metabolic disorders particular to the infant, digestive system disorders of the newborn, conditions impacting the newborn's integument and temperature control, other newborn problems, and other perinatal disorders (American Association of Professional Coders, 2022a).

9.17 Congenital Malformations, Deformations, and Chromosomal Abnormalities: Q00–Q99

The range Q00–Q99 includes ICD-10 codes for nervous system, circulatory system, respiratory system, and eye, ear, neck, and facial malformations. It also includes codes for cleft lip and palate, other digestive system congenital malformations, and genital organ congenital malformations. Q60–Q99 cover congenital urinary malformations, musculoskeletal malformations and deformations, other congenital malformations, and chromosomal abnormalities not otherwise classified (American Association of Professional Coders, 2022d).

9.18 Symptoms, Signs, and Abnormal Clinical and Laboratory Findings, Not Elsewhere Classified: R00–R99

ICD codes for symptoms and signs affecting the circulatory and respiratory systems are included in Symptoms, signs, and abnormal clinical and laboratory findings, not otherwise classified. It also encompasses signs and symptoms related to the digestive system and abdomen, the skin and subcutaneous tissue, as well as the nervous and musculoskeletal systems. This range also includes symptoms and signs concerning the genitourinary system, cognition, perception, emotional state, behavior, speech, voice, and general signs and symptoms. R70–R99 cover abnormal findings on analysis of blood, urine, and other bodily fluids, substances, and tissues that are not diagnosed. As well as abnormal findings on diagnostic imaging and function studies (without diagnosis), abnormal tumor markers, and an ill-defined and unclear cause of death (American Association of Professional Coders, 2022v).

9.19 Injury, Poisoning, and Certain Other Consequences of External Causes: S00–T88

This code range includes ICD-10 codes for head, neck, thorax, abdomen, lower back, lumbar spine, pelvis, and external genitals injuries. Injuries to the shoulder, upper arm, forearm, elbow, wrist, hand, fingers, hip, thigh, knee, lower leg, ankle, and foot are also included. T07–T88 encompass injury, poisoning, and certain other consequences of external causes (American Association of Professional Coders, 2022r).

What is the code set for diseases in the genitourinary system?

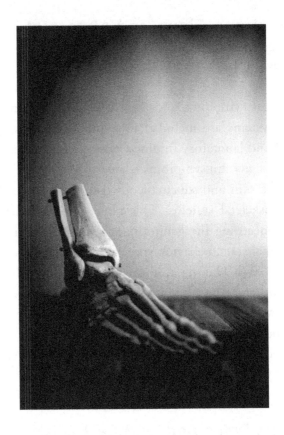

9.20 Codes for Special Purposes: U00-U85

ICD-10 codes are included in the "Codes for Special Purposes" section and can be used in emergencies or for newly discovered diseases with unknown etiology (American Association of Professional Coders, 2022c).

> What is included in ICD-10 code set O60-09A?

9.21 External Causes of Morbidity: V00–Y99

Accidents, deliberate self-harm, assault, and events of unknown motive are all examples of external causes of morbidity. As well as legal intervention, war operations, military exercises, and terrorism. This range also includes complications of medical and surgical care, as well as supplementary variables connected to morbidity causes classified elsewhere (American Association of Professional Coders, 2022p).

9.22 Factors Influencing Health Status and Contact with Health Services: Z00–Z99

Factors influencing health status and access to healthcare services include ICD-10 codes for people who need health services for examinations, genetic carriers and susceptibility to disease, and anti-microbial drug resistance. It also covers estrogen receptor status, remaining foreign body fragments, hormone sensitivity, malignancy status, and people who are at risk of communicable diseases. This range also includes codes for people experiencing health services in circumstances connected to reproduction, encounters for other specific health care, and people with possible health risks due to socioeconomic and psychological circumstances. Z66–Z99 encompass do not resuscitate status, blood type, body mass index (BMI), persons experiencing health services in other circumstances, and persons with potential health threats due to family and personal history, as well as specific variables influencing health status (American Association of Professional Coders, 2022q).

Formative Assessment Questions:

1. When are ophthalmological service codes 92002–92142 used?

2. What is the purpose of determination of refractive state services?

3. Which coding guidelines are used as the foundation for disease recording and statistics in primary, secondary, and tertiary care?

4. E00–E89 ICD codes cover diseases relating to which bodily system?

5. How are schizophrenia and other non-mood psychotic disorders coded?

Key Concepts

ICD-10-CM coding guidelines are as follows:
- Infectious and parasitic diseases: **A00–B99**

- Neoplasms: **C00–D49**

- Diseases of the blood and blood-forming organs and certain disorders involving the immune mechanism: **D50–D89**

- Endocrine, nutritional, and metabolic diseases: **E00–E89**

- Mental, behavioral, and neurodevelopmental disorders: **F01–F99**

- Diseases of the nervous system: **G00–G99**

- Diseases of the eye and adnexa: **H00–H59**

- Diseases of the ear and mastoid process: **H60–H95**

- Diseases of the circulatory system: **I00–I99**

- Diseases of the respiratory system: **J00–J99**

- Diseases of the digestive system: **K00–K95**

- Diseases of the skin and subcutaneous tissue: **L00–L99**

- Diseases of the musculoskeletal system and connective tissue: **M00–M99**

- Diseases of the genitourinary system: **N00–N99**

- Pregnancy, childbirth, and the puerperium: **O00–O9A**

- Conditions originating in the perinatal period: **P00–P96**

- Congenital malformations, deformations, and chromosomal abnormalities: **Q00–Q99**

- Symptoms, signs, and abnormal clinical and laboratory findings not classified elsewhere: **R00–R99**

- Injury, poisoning, and certain other consequences of external causes: **S00–T88**

- Emergencies or newly discovered diseases: **U00-U85**

- External causes of morbidity: **V00–Y99**

- Factors influencing health status and contact with health services: **Z00–Z99**

CHAPTER 10:

COMPLIANCE AND REGULATORY

Coding compliance is the process of ensuring that all coding rules, laws, and guidelines are followed while coding diagnoses, procedures, and data. A compliance plan should be in place at all provider offices and healthcare facilities. Internal controls in the claims and billing operations' reimbursement, coding, and payment sections are frequently the source of fraud and abuse and have been the target of government laws (Empire Provider News, 2020).

The Health Insurance Portability and Accountability Act of 1996 (HIPAA) is one such regulation. It is a federal law that required the development of national standards to secure sensitive patient health information from being disclosed without the patient's consent or knowledge (Centers for Disease Control and Prevention, 2019).

10.1 Medical Records Documentation

All medical record entries, including the provider's legible identification and date of service, should be comprehensive and legible. Each medical record encounter must include the patient's full name and date of birth. When there is incorrect information on the wrong patient health record, documentation integrity is jeopardized because it might impair clinical decision-making and patient safety. The signatures and credentials of providers are critical in any documentation initiatives. The signature is an affirmation that the treating and documenting provider has read and agreed to the written statement and that it appropriately reflects their intentions for the services provided during the encounter and their purpose(s) for scheduling the visit. Each time a patient goes for medical care, certain information is required to characterize the patient's experience. Each encounter should typically include the following:

- The main grievance
- The present illness's history
- The examination of the body
- Assessment and treatment plan (Empire Provider News, 2020)

10.2 Common Coding and Billing Risk Areas

The following billing issues are frequently investigated and audited by the Office of Inspector General (OIG):

- Billing for commodities or services that were not given or provided as stated
- Duplicate payment due to double billing
- Submitting claims for non-reasonable and unnecessary equipment, medical supplies, and services
- Non-covered services billing
- Intentionally abusing provider identification numbers, resulting in incorrect billing
- Unbundling
- Failure to employ modifiers correctly
- Upcoding the service level (Empire Provider News, 2020)

E/M claims are often refused for two reasons: improper coding (the code does not match the paperwork) and insufficient documentation (a lack of provider signature or no record of the scope and duration of time spent in counseling). The second reason is for care coordination when it is used to qualify for a specific level of E/M service. There are various methods for preventing E/M claims from being denied: Providers should assess whether the service is acceptable and necessary in addition to the particular requirements for billing a chosen E/M code (for example, a level 5 office visit for a patient with a common cold and no comorbidities will not be reasonable and necessary). When choosing codes for E/M services, keep the following in mind:

- Type of patient (new or established)
- Service location/setting

- The level of service provided is determined by the extent of the history, the scope of the examination, and the complexity of the medical decision-making process (for example, the number and type of the key components performed) (Empire Provider News, 2020)

Best Practices to Avoid Common Documentation Mistakes

For each interaction, providers must develop a thorough and accurate description of the patient's condition, as well as a detailed plan of care. Listing difficulties without a plan of care does not confirm medical management of that problem and may result in a reduction in complexity. Listing concerns with a short, generalized comment (for example, diabetes management (DM), chronic kidney disease (CKD), congestive heart failure (CHF): Continue present treatment plan) reduces the physician's complexity and effort (Empire Provider News, 2020).

The care plan must be well-defined. The care plan represents problems that the physician personally manages, as well as those that must be considered when he or she develops management alternatives, even if the problem is largely managed by another provider. One provider, for example, can oversee the patient's diabetic treatment while the nephrologist manages the chronic kidney disease (CKD). Pathology, laboratory testing, radiography, and medicine-based diagnostic tests all help to diagnose and manage patient problems (Empire Provider News, 2020).

Some pointers to keep in mind when documenting: identify the tests ordered and write the rationale in the medical record. Next, include a description of the test review in the note (for example, elevated glucose levels). Then, when images, tracings, or specimens are personally evaluated, provide feedback on the results. Finally, briefly describe any discussions with the physician performing the operation or diagnostic study about unexpected or contradictory test results (Empire Provider News, 2020).

Based on the presenting problem, diagnostic procedures required, and management options chosen, patients' risk in E/M is classified as minimum, low, moderate, or high. Chronic disorders with exacerbations and invasive procedures pose a greater danger to patients than acute, simple illnesses or non-invasive procedures. Stable or improving problems are considered less dangerous than progressive problems; conditions that threaten life/bodily function outweigh undiagnosed problems where the patient's prognosis is uncertain (Empire Provider News, 2020).

Do not assume that the auditor or coder can deduce the appropriate complexity of the patient's problems from the documentation specifics; instead, providers should note the status of all problems in the plan of care and categorize them as stable, worsening, or progressing (mild or severe), as necessary. Document all diagnostic or therapeutic procedures explored, and, when relevant, identify surgical risk factors involving comorbid disorders that put the patient at greater risk than the average patient (Empire Provider News, 2020).

Medical coding compliance requires frequent auditing. To ensure that your organization's E/M services are properly coded, it is critical to review your charts on a regular basis to look for insufficient documentation, miscoding, upcoding, and downcoding. Auditing your medical coding process and practices can help you identify recurring risk areas and important improvement opportunities. Using these insights, you may implement best practices and rectify any problematic habits, reducing the likelihood of negative consequences (Empire Provider News, 2020).

10.3 Topics That Could Be Covered in the CPC Exam

The CPC exam's compliance and regulatory section has five questions but there are more than five categories in this section. This information is not contained in your manuals but it is common knowledge among those who operate in the industry. The categories include Medicare Parts A, B, C, and D services, payment policy coding, place of service reporting, and fraud and abuse. NCCI edits, NCD/LCD, HIPAA, ABNs, and RVUs are also included in this section (Jandroep, 2018).

CCI or NCCI Edits

The National Correct Coding Initiative (NCCI) was created by the Centers for Medicare & Medicaid Services (CMS) to promote national correct coding methodologies and to manage faulty coding that could lead to incorrect payment in Part B claims. The NCCI program is owned by the CMS, which is responsible for all content decisions. The CMS based its coding requirements on the American Medical Association's CPT Manual, national and local policies and edits, national society coding guidelines, a review of conventional medical and surgical practices, and an evaluation of existing coding methods. The CMS annually updates the National Correct

Coding Initiative Policy Manual for Medicare Services. Medicare Administrative Contractors (MACs) should use the NCCI Policy Manual as a basic reference tool that explains the rationale for NCCI edits (Centers for Medicare & Medicaid Services, 2022b).

National Coverage Determinations (NCD)/ Local Coverage Determinations (LCD)

Medicare coverage is restricted to reasonable and required items and services for a patient's injury or illness (and within the scope of a Medicare benefit category). National coverage determinations (NCDs) are determined using an evidence-based approach that includes chances for public input. CMS's internal research is supplemented in some cases by an outside technology evaluation and/or collaboration with the Medicare Evidence Development & Coverage Advisory Committee (MEDCAC). A Medicare contractor may cover an item or service based on a local coverage determination (LCD) when there is a lack of a national coverage policy (Centers for Medicare & Medicaid Services, 2022a).

Advanced Beneficiary Notice (ABN)

The ABN (Advanced Beneficiary Notice) is a document that is sent to Medicare patients even before receiving a service that is unlikely to be covered by Medicare. The notice shows that the service will not be covered, and the patient agrees to pay the charges for the service(s) himself. An ABN is typically used when medical necessity is not fulfilled but the doctor and patient still wish to proceed with the service with the patient fully aware of the expenses and accepting responsibility for them (Jandroep, 2015).

Relative Value Units (RVUs)

RVUs are the foundation of the Resource-Based Relative Value Scale (RBRVS), a system used to assess physician payment by the CMS and private payers. RVUs, or relative value units, do not describe physician compensation in monetary terms. RVUs define the value of a service or procedure in relation to all other services and procedures. This metric is based on the amount of physician labor, clinical and non-clinical resources, and knowledge required to provide patients with healthcare. When the conversion factor (CF) and dollars per RVU is added to the total RVU, the result is physician income (American Academy of Professional Coders, 2022).

The RBRVS determines physician payment for services as follows:

- Total RVUs
- Geographic Practice Cost Indices (GPCIs)
- Conversion Factor (CF)

Note: Please keep in mind that some CPT® codes take into account other elements, which CMS defines as professional or technical component (TC) fees (American Academy of Professional Coders, 2022).

Types of RVUs

The RBRVS model employs three distinct components, or categories of RVUs, that, when totaled, determine payment in order to precisely capture the consumption of time, effort, and money required in providing a service to patients. These RVU types are used to measure the following:

- Work RVUs record the provider's time spent conducting a procedure or providing a service. Technical skills, physical effort, mental effort and judgment, stress connected to patient risk, and the length of time required to provide the service or treatment are all factors in this value. Work RVUs account for 50.866 % of a code's total RVU.

- RVUs for practice expenses (PE) reflect the cost of clinical and non-clinical labor as well as practice expenses. Medical and office supplies, clinical and administrative staff, and pro rata expenditures of building space, utilities, medical equipment, and office equipment are all included. Practice expense RVUs account for 44.839 % of a service's total RVU.

- Malpractice (MP) RVUs show the cost of professional liability insurance according to a risk assessment for each CPT® code. Malpractice RVUs add up to 4.295% of total RVUs for a service.

CMS modifies physician work, practice costs, and professional liability insurance relative values yearly to accommodate changes in medicine, technology, and the economy, based on recommendations by the AMA's Specialty Society Relative Value Scale Update Committee (RUC). RUC also evaluates new, amended, and potentially misvalued codes each year in order to determine a relative value by comparing physician work to existing codes. CMS is required by statute to review all components of the RBRVS at least every five years (American Academy of Professional Coders, 2022).

Note: Although Medicare has its own payer systems and procedures, most non-Medicare payers, including private health plans, use the

RBRVS as a baseline to determine payments (American Academy of Professional Coders, 2022).

Why Are RVUs Important to Understand?

Understanding how the relative values of medical services translate into fee schedule payment amounts can help medical practices and healthcare organizations better anticipate and address yearly changes that will have an impact on their bottom line. Changes in RVU assignments have varying effects on practices, depending on the number of services provided and the volume of operations performed (American Academy of Professional Coders, 2022).

Medicare Parts A, B, C, and D Services

Medicare services are divided into four parts: A, B, C, and D. Part A covers inpatient/hospital care, Part B covers outpatient/medical care, Part C gives an alternative method of receiving Medicare benefits, and Part D covers prescription drugs. In general, the various components of Medicare help in the coverage of certain services. The majority of recipients elect to get their Part A and B benefits through Original Medicare, the conventional fee-for-service program provided directly by the federal government. Traditional Medicare is often referred to as Fee-for-Service Medicare (FFS). The government directly pays for the healthcare services you receive through Original Medicare. You can see any doctor or hospital in the country who accepts Medicare (and most do) (American Academy of Professional Coders, 2022).

In Original Medicare:

- When you require medical attention, you go directly to the doctor or hospital. There is no need to obtain prior permission/authorization from Medicare or your healthcare physician.

- Part B requires you to pay a monthly fee. Some people pay an additional fee for Part A.

- You usually have to pay a coinsurance fee for each service you receive.

- The fees that doctors and hospitals can charge for your care are limited

In most circumstances, if you want prescription medication coverage with Original Medicare, you must actively choose and join a stand-alone Medicare private drug plan (PDP).

Note: If you fulfill the eligibility conditions, there are a number of government programs that may help you lower your healthcare and prescription drug expenditures (American Academy of Professional Coders, 2022).

Formative Assessment Questions:

1. Where would the codes for cerebral palsy and other paralytic syndromes be found?

2. What are three diseases of the ear and mastoid processes included in the ICD-10 code set?

3. What is coding compliance?

4. What is the purpose of the HIPAA?

5. When a patient seeks medical care, what information should be recorded during each encounter?

Key Concepts

- **Coding compliance** is the process of ensuring that all coding rules, laws, and guidelines are followed while coding diagnoses, procedures, and data.

- The **Health Insurance Portability and Accountability Act of 1996 (HIPAA)** is a federal law that required the development of national standards to secure sensitive patient health information from being disclosed without the patient's consent or knowledge.

- E/M claims are often refused for two reasons: **improper coding** and **insufficient documentation.**

- Best practices to avoid common documentation mistakes are as follows:

  - Providers must develop a thorough and accurate description of the patient's condition and a detailed plan of care.

  - The care plan must be well-defined.

  - Do not assume that the auditor or coder can deduce the appropriate complexity of the patient's problems from the documentation specifics.

  - Providers should note the status of all problems in the plan of care and categorize them as necessary.

  - Review your charts on a regular basis to look for insufficient documentation, miscoding, upcoding, and downcoding.

- Possible topics in the CPC exam include **CCI or NCCI edits, National Coverage Determinations (NCD)/Local Coverage Determinations (LCD), Advanced Beneficiary Notice (ABN), Relative Value Units (RVUs), Medicare Parts A, B, C, and D Services.**

- The **National Correct Coding Initiative (NCCI)** was created by the Centers for Medicare & Medicaid Services (CMS) to promote national correct coding methodologies and to manage faulty coding that could lead to incorrect payment in Part B claims.

- **National coverage determinations (NCDs)** are determined using an evidence-based approach that includes chances for public input.

- The **Advanced Beneficiary Notice** is a document that is sent to Medicare patients even before receiving a service that is unlikely to be covered by Medicare.

- **Relative Value Units** are the foundation of the Resource-Based Relative Value Scale (RBRVS), a system used to assess physician payment by the CMS and private payers.

- Medicare services are divided into four parts: A, B, C, and D. Part A covers inpatient/hospital care, Part B covers outpatient/medical care, Part C gives an alternative method of receiving Medicare benefits, and Part D covers prescription drugs.

REFERENCES

AAPC. (2019). *CPC exam - certified professional coder - medical coding certification.* AAPC. https://www.aapc.com/certification/cpc/

AAPC. (2021, November 18). *Tips to pass the CPC exam in 2022.* AAPC.com. https://www.aapc.com/training/study-tips-to-pass-cpc-exam.aspx

AAPC. (2022, January 20). *How to pass the CPC exam in 2022.* AAPC.com. https://www.aapc.com/training/tips-to-take-the-cpc-exam.aspx

American Academy of Professional Coders. (2022, June 21). *What are RVUs?* AAPC.com. https://www.aapc.com/practice-management/rvus.aspx

American Association of Professional Coders. (2022a). *Certain conditions originating in the perinatal period - ICD-10 codes.* AAPC.com. https://www.aapc.com/codes/icd-10-codes-range/P00-P96/

American Association of Professional Coders. (2022b). *Certain infectious and parasitic diseases - ICD-10 codes.* AAPC.com. https://www.aapc.com/codes/icd-10-codes-range/A00-B99/

American Association of Professional Coders. (2022c). *Codes for special purposes- ICD-10 codes*. AAPC.com. https://www.aapc.com/codes/icd-10-codes-range/U00-U85/

American Association of Professional Coders. (2022d). *Congenital malformations, deformations and chromosomal abnormalities - ICD-10 codes*. AAPC.com. https://www.aapc.com/codes/icd-10-codes-range/Q00-Q99/

American Association of Professional Coders. (2022e). *Diseases of the blood and blood-forming organs and certain disorders involving the immune mechanism - ICD-10 codes*. AAPC.com. https://www.aapc.com/codes/icd-10-codes-range/D50-D89/

American Association of Professional Coders. (2022f). *Diseases of the circulatory system - ICD-10 codes*. AAPC.com. https://www.aapc.com/codes/icd-10-codes-range/I00-I99/

American Association of Professional Coders. (2022g). *Diseases of the digestive system - ICD-10 codes*. AAPC.com. https://www.aapc.com/codes/icd-10-codes-range/K00-K95/

American Association of Professional Coders. (2022h). *Diseases of the ear and mastoid process - ICD-10 codes*. AAPC.com. https://www.aapc.com/codes/icd-10-codes-range/H60-H95/

American Association of Professional Coders. (2022i). *Diseases of the eye and adnexa - ICD-10 codes*. AAPC.com. https://www.aapc.com/codes/icd-10-codes-range/H00-H59/

American Association of Professional Coders. (2022j). *Diseases of the genitourinary system - ICD-10 codes*. AAPC.

com.   https://www.aapc.com/codes/icd-10-codes-range/
N00-N99/

American Association of Professional Coders. (2022k).
*Diseases of the musculoskeletal system and connective tissue -
ICD-10 codes.* AAPC.com. https://www.aapc.com/codes/
icd-10-codes-range/M00-M99/

American Association of Professional Coders. (2022l).
Diseases of the nervous system - ICD-10 codes. AAPC.com.
https://www.aapc.com/codes/icd-10-codes-range/G00-G99/

American Association of Professional Coders. (2022m).
Diseases of the respiratory system - ICD-10 codes. AAPC.com.
https://www.aapc.com/codes/icd-10-codes-range/J00-J99/

American Association of Professional Coders. (2022n).
*Diseases of the skin and subcutaneous tissue - ICD-
10 codes.* AAPC.com. https://www.aapc.com/codes/
icd-10-codes-range/L00-L99/

American Association of Professional Coders. (2022o).
*Endocrine, nutritional and metabolic diseases - ICD-
10 codes.* AAPC.com. https://www.aapc.com/codes/
icd-10-codes-range/E00-E89/

American Association of Professional Coders. (2022p).
External causes of morbidity - ICD-10 codes. AAPC.com.
https://www.aapc.com/codes/icd-10-codes-range/V00-Y99/

American Association of Professional Coders. (2022q).
*Factors influencing health status and contact with health ser-
vices - ICD-10 codes.* AAPC.com. https://www.aapc.com/
codes/icd-10-codes-range/Z00-Z99/

American Association of Professional Coders. (2022r). *Injury, poisoning and certain other consequences of external causes - ICD-10 codes-*. AAPC.com. https://www.aapc.com/codes/icd-10-codes-range/S00-T88/

American Association of Professional Coders. (2022s). *Mental, behavioral and neurodevelopmental disorders - ICD-10 codes*. AAPC.com. https://www.aapc.com/codes/icd-10-codes-range/F01-F99/

American Association of Professional Coders. (2022t). *Neoplasms - ICD-10 codes*. AAPC.com. https://www.aapc.com/codes/icd-10-codes-range/C00-D49/

American Association of Professional Coders. (2022u). *Pregnancy, childbirth and the puerperium - ICD-10 codes*. AAPC.com. https://www.aapc.com/codes/icd-10-codes-range/O00-O9A/

American Association of Professional Coders. (2022v). *Symptoms, signs and abnormal clinical and laboratory findings, not elsewhere classified - ICD-10 codes*. AAPC.com. https://www.aapc.com/codes/icd-10-codes-range/R00-R99/

American Medical Association. (2022). Evaluation and management services guide. In *Centers for Medicare and Medicaid Services* (pp. 4–20). https://www.cms.gov/outreach-and-education/medicare-learning-network-mln/mlnproducts/downloads/eval-mgmt-serv-guide-icn006764.pdf

American Society of Anesthesiologists. (2022a). *Anesthesia 101: What is anesthesia?* American Society of Anesthesiologists | Made for This Moment. https://www.asahq.org/madeforthismoment/anesthesia-101/

American Society of Anesthesiologists. (2022b). *Anesthesia risks and assessment.* American Society of Anesthesiologists | Made for This Moment. https://www.asahq.org/madeforthismoment/anesthesia-101/anesthesia-risks/

American Society of Anesthesiologists. (2022c). *Effects of anesthesia on brain & body.* American Society of Anesthesiologists | Made for This Moment. https://www.asahq.org/madeforthismoment/anesthesia-101/effects-of-anesthesia/

American Society of Anesthesiologists. (2022d). *General anesthesia: Definition & side effects.* American Society of Anesthesiologists | Made for This Moment. https://www.asahq.org/madeforthismoment/anesthesia-101/types-of-anesthesia/general-anesthesia/

American Society of Anesthesiologists. (2022e). *IV sedation: Definition & effects.* American Society of Anesthesiologists | Made for This Moment. https://www.asahq.org/madeforthismoment/anesthesia-101/types-of-anesthesia/ivmonitored-sedation/

American Society of Anesthesiologists. (2022f). *Local anesthesia: Definition & effects.* American Society of Anesthesiologists | Made for This Moment. https://www.asahq.org/madeforthismoment/anesthesia-101/types-of-anesthesia/local-anesthesia/

American Society of Anesthesiologists. (2022g). *Regional anesthesia: Definition & effects.* American Society of Anesthesiologists | Made for This Moment. https://www.asahq.org/madeforthismoment/anesthesia-101/types-of-anesthesia/regional-anesthesia/

Bernard, S. P., Netter, F. H., & American Medical Association. (2015). *Netter's atlas of surgical anatomy for CPT coding*. American Medical Association.

Centers for Disease Control and Prevention. (2019, February 21). *Health insurance portability and accountability act of 1996 (HIPAA)*. CDC.gov. https://www.cdc.gov/phlp/publications/topic/hipaa.html#:~:text=The%20Health%20Insurance%20Portability%20and

Centers for Medicare & Medicaid Services. (2022a, March 3). *Medicare coverage determination process*. CMS.gov. https://www.cms.gov/Medicare/Coverage/DeterminationProcess

Centers for Medicare & Medicaid Services. (2022b, October 6). *National correct coding initiative edits*. CMS.gov. https://www.cms.gov/Medicare/Coding/NCCI-Coding-Edits

Cleveland Clinic. (2020, December 5). *Endocrine system: What is it, functions & organs*. Cleveland Clinic. https://my.clevelandclinic.org/health/articles/21201-endocrine-system

Empire Provider News. (2020, November). *Coding spotlight: Tips and best practices for compliance*. Providernews.empireblue.com. https://providernews.empireblue.com/article/coding-spotlight-tips-and-best-practices-for-compliance-3

Green, M. A. (2010). *3-2-1 code it!* (2nd ed.). Delmar, Cengage Learning.

Health Images. (2020, February 21). *What is radiology?* Health Images. https://www.healthimages.com/what-is-radiology/

Hulme, A. (2021, July 5). *What is the passing score on the AAPC CPC exam?* PopularAsk.net. https://popularask.net/what-is-the-passing-score-on-the-aapc-cpc-exam/

Inside Radiology. (2016a, September 12). *Diagnostic radiology.* Inside Radiology. https://www.insideradiology.com.au/diagnostic-radiology/

Inside Radiology. (2016b, September 23). *Radiation oncology.* Inside Radiology. https://www.insideradiology.com.au/radiation-oncology/

Inside Radiology. (2016c, October 14). *Musculoskeletal imaging.* Inside Radiology. https://www.insideradiology.com.au/musculoskeletal-imaging/

Inside Radiology. (2016d, November 17). *Breast imaging.* Inside Radiology. https://www.insideradiology.com.au/breast-imaging/

Inside Radiology. (2016e, November 21). *Cardiac imaging.* Inside Radiology. https://www.insideradiology.com.au/cardiac-imaging/

Inside Radiology. (2017, August 31). *Abdominal imaging.* Inside Radiology. https://www.insideradiology.com.au/abdominal-imaging/

Inside Radiology. (2018, October 4). *Interventional radiology.* Inside Radiology. https://www.insideradiology.com.au/interventional-radiology/

Jandroep, L. (2015, February 23). *What is ABN or advanced beneficiary notice?* Certification

Coaching Organization LLC. https://www.cco.us/medical-billers-advanced-beneficiary-notices/

Jandroep, L. (2018, January 30). *Compliance and regulatory questions on CPC® exam.* Youtube.com. https://www.youtube.com/watch?v=CsfNskW8LUw

Medical Billing and Coding. (2021, February 2). *CPC exam: Pathology and laboratory.* Medical Billing and Coding. https://www.medicalbillingandcoding.org/cpc-exam-pathology-laboratory/

Medical Billing and Coding. (2022, June 8). *CPC exam: General preparation and test strategies.* MedicalBillingandCoding.org. https://www.medicalbillingandcoding.org/general-preparation-test-strategies-cpc-exam/

World Health Organisation. (2022). *Classification of Diseases (ICD).* World Health Organisation (WHO). https://www.who.int/standards/classifications/classification-of-diseases

World Health Organization. (2016). ICD-10 Volume 2. In *World Health Organization (WHO)* (pp. 3, 14–15, 28–29). https://icd.who.int/browse10/Content/statichtml/ICD10Volume2_en_2019.pdf

Zippia. (2020a, October 2). *How to become a certified professional coder in 2022: Step by step guide and career paths.* Zippia. https://www.zippia.com/certified-professional-coder-jobs/

Zippia. (2020b, October 2). *What does a certified professional coder do.* Zippia. https://www.zippia.com/certified-professional-coder-jobs/what-does-a-certified-professional-coder-do/

IMAGE REFERENCE

blickpixel. (n.d.). Hospital hallway waiting room [Image]. In *Pixabay.com*. Retrieved August 12, 2022, from https://pixabay.com/photos/hospital-hallway-waiting-room-floor-502885/

Calvert, A. (2021). Muscular anatomical torso [Image]. In *Unsplash.com*. https://unsplash.com/photos/DuEHkSHvXUQ

CDC. (2020). X-ray showing pneumonia [Image]. In *Unsplash.com*. https://unsplash.com/photos/SrHKQxGuuqQ

Chernaya, K. (2020). Ophthalmologist checking eyesight [Image]. In *Pexels.com*. https://www.pexels.com/photo/unrecognizable-ophthalmologist-checking-eyesight-of-woman-on-vision-screener-5765827/

Clker-Free-Vector-Images. (n.d.-a). Brain diagram medical [Image]. In *Pixabay.com*. Retrieved August 12, 2022, from https://pixabay.com/vectors/brain-diagram-medical-biology-40356/

Clker-Free-Vector-Images. (n.d.-b). Digestive system [Image]. In *Pixabay.com*. Retrieved August 12, 2022, from https://pixabay.com/vectors/digestion-intestine-digestive-oral-303364/

Clker-Free-Vector-Images. (n.d.-c). Eye diagram eyeball [Image]. In *Pixabay.com*. Retrieved August 12, 2022, from https://pixabay.com/vectors/eye-diagram-eyeball-body-pupil-39998/

cottonbro. (2020). Medical imaging of the brain [Image]. In *Pexals.com*. https://www.pexels.com/photo/medical-imaging-of-the-brain-5723875/

Czerwinski, P. (2018). Microscope [Image]. In *Unsplash.com*. https://unsplash.com/photos/JdtUKqGdqw8

Grabowska, K. (2020). Close up photo of syringe needle [Image]. In *Pexels.com*. https://www.pexels.com/photo/close-up-photo-of-syringe-needle-4047185/

Hutton, N. (2020). Woman in white tube top [Image]. In *unsplash.com*. https://unsplash.com/photos/AjU6Z5k_uBI

James, L. (2020). Crop black physician writing on paper document at work [Image]. In *Pexels.com*. https://www.pexels.com/photo/crop-black-physician-writing-on-paper-document-at-work-6097759/

Mart Production. (2021). MRI machine [Image]. In *Pexels.com*. https://www.pexels.com/photo/person-technology-room-health-7089390/

Norin, O. (2021a). Closeup of skeleton foot model [Image]. In *Unsplash.com*. https://unsplash.com/photos/FAdw0aRMXp4

Norin, O. (2021b). Closeup of skeleton pelvic model [Image]. In *Unsplash.com*. https://unsplash.com/photos/xqPhcfPO0jc

Ramos, M. (2020). Anesthesia drug infusion [Image]. In *Unsplash.com*. https://unsplash.com/photos/m9617OjWgoM

Roma, A. (2021). Cheek and piercing in ear of crop black woman [Image]. In *Pexels.com*. https://www.pexels.com/photo/cheek-and-piercing-in-ear-of-crop-black-woman-7480268/

Roy, M. (2021). Stethosscope [Image]. In *Unsplash.com*. https://unsplash.com/photos/u7GtZ0yVijw

Shvets, A. (2020). A doctor holding an x-ray result [Image]. In *Pexels.com*. https://www.pexels.com/photo/a-doctor-holding-an-x-ray-result-4226258/

Weermeijer, R. (2018). Open heart model [Image]. In *Unsplash.com*. https://unsplash.com/photos/Tmkwl7EjVtE

DOWNLOAD YOUR FREE E-BOOK

As our way of thanking you for purchasing the **Study and Exam Guide of Certified Professional Coder (CPC)**, you'll get the **Three Highly Effective Test-Taking Strategies According to My Research** for free! This e-book features three research-supported strategies combining mental, emotional, and behavioral practices for successful test performance and outcome.

To get your free e-book, kindly go to https://thegeniusexamcoaches.com/CPC to receive the download instructions.

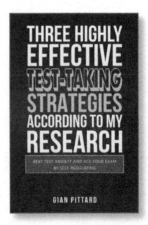

WE'D LIKE TO HEAR FROM YOU

The publisher invites you to share your
feedback by leaving a review on our page.

We value your thoughts and testimonies as we continue
to write high-quality study and exam guides to help our
readers succeed in their careers and life in general.

Made in the USA
Las Vegas, NV
17 February 2024